PATHS *of* PIONEER CHRISTIAN SCIENTISTS

PATHS *of* PIONEER CHRISTIAN SCIENTISTS

Christopher L. Tyner

Edited by Stephen R. Howard

Longyear Museum Press
Chestnut Hill, Massachusetts, U.S.A.

This book was designed by Karen Shea of Karen Shea Design.
The book was printed and bound by Kase Printing, Inc., in Hudson, N.H.
Kase Printing is an FSC-certified printer using soy-based inks and Renewable
Energy Credits in their production facility.

The text face is Minion, designed by Robert Slimbach
for Adobe Systems in 1989. The remaining typeface is Syntax,
designed by Swiss typeface designer Hans Meier in 1968.

Longyear Museum Press
1125 Boylston Street
Chestnut Hill, MA, U.S.A. 02467-1811
800-277-8943
www.longyear.org

TABLE OF CONTENTS

FOREWORD   vii

PREFACE   ix

EMMA A. THOMPSON   1

ABIGAIL DYER THOMPSON   39

JANETTE E. WELLER   67

ANNIE MACMILLAN KNOTT   89

NOTES   131

FOREWORD

Here are narratives of people who had come to a crisis in their lives, a seeming dead end. At the critical moment, however, each found that Christian Science opened the door of healing. They could, like so many others, have simply chalked the healing up to a miraculous intervention, an interruption of the daily routine, and gone comfortably back to that routine.

But the door of healing had opened onto a view of spiritual beauty, awesome in its rugged freshness, compelling in its promise, as gentle and inviting as it was stern and commanding. The four people who are the subjects of this book accepted the invitation of this beauty and stepped across the threshold, out of conventions and onto paths of exploration and high adventure.

From time to time we are asked why four *women* were chosen as the subjects of this book. Several criteria determined selection: the available historical evidence, the range of a person's contributions to the history of Christian Science, the relative familiarity of that person among today's Christian Scientists (Abigail Dyer Thompson, for instance, is familiar to readers of *We Knew Mary Baker Eddy,* while her mother, Emma A. Thompson, at one time known throughout the Christian Science field for her remarkable healing work, is largely unknown today). At the outset of the research and writing it was not our intention to restrict the book to women, but as the work progressed, these four people showed striking similarities and contrasts, which were heightened by considering them together. We anticipate a future Longyear publication will present stories of several men engaged in the pioneering work.

There are of course many people, perhaps hundreds, who lived during the first fifty years of Christian Science whose life stories deserve to be told but who are unknown to us today simply because the historical evidence has not survived. We know of a healing or an event only if evidence about it has come down to us. A technical matter should here be noted: in a few instances spelling and punctuation in the historical documents have been silently corrected in the following accounts.

Reminiscences present valuable clues to the past, but they have limitations: they can conceal, intentionally or inadvertently, as much as they disclose; they are sometimes sketchy, collapsing long periods of time and complex events into a few sentences, and too often ignore critical junctures all together. One example will serve: Abigail Dyer Thompson was about eight years old when she met Mary Baker Eddy, and a friendship between the two developed (what other teenager would routinely be invited to Pleasant View for personal visits with the Discoverer of Christian Science?). But what did it mean to Miss Thompson when this special friend and teacher passed on in 1910, followed by the passing of Miss Thompson's mother and co-worker just three years later? Did these events, which marked the end of an era, mean that her pioneering days had ended, or did Miss Thompson find that the work continued to require the same degree of rugged stalwartness as before? How much of the pioneering spirit did she draw upon during the next five decades? Her reminiscence is silent about these questions. That she continued her work as practitioner and teacher until the late 1950s is a fact. But after 1907 we have only occasional glimpses of Miss Thompson herself, what she thought, what she felt, and we know almost nothing about her younger sister, Ella, who also was active in Christian Science work.

Christopher L. Tyner, through countless close perusals of the documentary evidence concerning the four pioneers of this book, set out on his own path of discovery as he patiently sorted, sifted, and evaluated. He has drawn from the raw material, from the disparate bits and pieces of evidence, the stories, themes, and qualities that make these people of such relevance today. He shows that in spite of having so much in common, each of these four women nonetheless has a unique story and voice, as well as a unique friendship with Mary Baker Eddy.

Each of these pioneers has something valuable to say to us today, and as these accounts demonstrate, each has earned the right to say it.

Stephen R. Howard

PREFACE

WHOEVER OPENS THE WAY IN CHRISTIAN SCIENCE IS A PILGRIM AND STRANGER, MARKING OUT THE PATH FOR GENERATIONS YET UNBORN.

— MARY BAKER EDDY, *SCIENCE AND HEALTH WITH KEY TO THE SCRIPTURES*

Jesus once told his disciples that their spiritual work was connected to the holy labors of those who had come before them. "I sent you to reap that whereon ye bestowed no labour," he told them as recorded in the fourth chapter of John. "Other men laboured, and ye are entered into their labours."

In this same way, Christian Scientists today have entered into the holy labors and selfless struggles of the Christian Scientists who came before them. Looking down the long corridor of history, today's Christian Scientists would see a continuity beginning with Mary Baker Eddy and her discovery of Christian Science and moving forward as some of her early students took a tiny seed of truth out from their teacher's classroom and planted it in the soil of their hometown. From the early efforts of these men and women, who took up the work of the first Christian Science practitioners to heal and help others, came the establishment of Christian Science in various localities, the organizing and building of churches, the opening of Reading Rooms, and more.

The four women whose stories occupy this book — Emma A. and Abigail Dyer Thompson, Janette E. Weller, and Annie M. Knott — were pioneers of the first order. A dictionary defines *pioneer* as "a person who goes before, preparing the way for others, as an early settler or a scientist doing exploratory work" (*Webster's New World Dictionary*). These women (and men) stood face to face with a sometimes dark and threatening wilderness. With no clear path before them they courageously set about to create one. Each step in this wilderness was, for them, a first step.

Our purpose in researching and writing this book is to honor the commitment, dedication, and accomplishments of these pioneer Christian

Scientists and to examine carefully how they did what they did. What were the specific ways they went about their work?

The reader will discover that three of the four pioneers in this book came to Christian Science after suffering in the wilderness of disease, pain, and sometimes agony. For Annie Knott it was the discovery that her son had swallowed a bottle of carbolic acid and doctors had rendered their verdict that he had twenty-four hours to live. For Emma Thompson it was a fight from the time of her childhood against a painful condition of neuralgia. For Janette Weller it was a twenty-year struggle with tuberculosis. And for the fourth pioneer, Abigail Dyer Thompson, it was being healed as a child, through Mrs. Eddy's own work, of serious health conditions, including severe lung trouble that reached back three generations.

Each woman was completely healed through Christian Science. But each considered the healing not an end but a beginning. Each of these four lives pivoted off the healing onto an entirely new life direction. Each spent the rest of her life showing others the path out of the wilderness. In this way, each pioneer has a unique story to tell of what it took to be counted among Mrs. Eddy's students. These are four adventure stories of people whose extraordinary courage, fierce dedication, and encompassing love stood up to the mental elements of their time and won the day.

We have many biographies of Mary Baker Eddy today. But the stories of pioneer Christian Scientists, for the most part, remain to be told. They sit quietly on thousands of pages of historical documents, letters, reminiscences and private papers — awaiting research and writing. It is remarkable, given what these pioneers have bestowed upon us, given how their lives have so directly affected our own, that we do not know more about them. It has been and is the purpose of Longyear Museum to help remedy this inequity with this volume and other publications.

There is sometimes a tendency to think of pioneer Christian Scientists as superwomen and supermen, filled with strength and wisdom unavailable today, somehow no longer within reach. In contrast, after years researching and writing these articles, I would argue that the genius of the pioneers lies in their willingness to realize, as Mrs. Eddy writes in *Science and Health,* "the inability of corporeality, as well as the infinite ability of Spirit" (p. 494).

At one time or another, most of these early workers were unsure of themselves, reluctant, left alone to wrestle with some shortcoming, to face their own "inability of corporeality" as they pressed forward in their efforts to represent Christian Science to a sometimes hostile public. Yet each would also learn to draw upon "the infinite ability of Spirit," enabling her to help and heal others.

Pioneer Annie M. Knott makes the arresting observation that each and every Christian Scientist, no matter of what era, is making history:

> *It would be interesting to know how many there are who appreciate the fact that we are all helping to make history, and how many estimate in any degree their obligation to posterity....*
>
> *In the vista of the past we behold the heroic characters who helped to determine the events of their day, and who thus made posterity their debtor. In no case do we find that any important step was taken, any great advance made save as the result of a mighty struggle between good and evil, —* Mind and materiality. [The Christian Science Journal, vol. 21 (*November 1903*), p. 514.]

I want to thank the Longyear Museum Trustees for their commitment, incredible patience, and never-failing support for this project. I also want to thank the book's editor, Stephen R. Howard, whose decades of study and scholarship of Mrs. Eddy and her history, earned by hard work and research at the Archives of The First Church of Christ, Scientist, and at Longyear Museum, proved a huge contribution to the finished book you have in your hand. I also greatly appreciate the encouragement of Longyear Museum's Executive Director, Anne H. McCauley, at every step of the way. She made available the time and resources to undertake this project, and her guidance was invaluable.

Sandra J. Houston's encouragement and support provided many cups of cold water along the journey, and Pamela S. Partridge's organizational skills kept the complex process on track and helped us across the finish line. I would like to thank the gracious staff of The Mary Baker Eddy Library for their assistance. Special thanks also go to the following members of the Longyear Museum staff: Catherine Hammond, whose skills in copyediting and meticulous checking of notes and sources have contributed much; Cheryl P. Moneyhun and Webster Lithgow, for their review of drafts and helpful suggestions; Michael D. Sylvester, for gathering images for these narratives; Natalie R. Mozzer, for her tireless and cheerful assistance with checking proof pages. Finally, great thanks also go to Karen Shea for her talents in design and her unfailing patience.

Christopher L. Tyner

EMMA A. THOMPSON

FAITHFUL OVER A FEW THINGS, RULER OVER MANY

Emma A. Thompson, C.S.D., circa 1885.
Photograph, Longyear Museum Collection.

EMMA A. THOMPSON

FAITHFUL OVER A FEW THINGS, RULER OVER MANY

BY THE TIME MINNESOTA SENATOR ALLEN J. GREER AROSE TO ADDRESS HIS STATE assembly, the future of Christian Science and its practice there in the 1890s hung precariously in the balance.

Inside the Minnesota State Capitol a contingent of assemblymen had already argued — in concert with the local medical community — that Mary Baker Eddy's new faith was dangerous. Indeed, they claimed, citizens of Minnesota needed a law to protect them from the harm that would come when Christian Scientists disobeyed the quarantine laws.

Then State Senator Greer arose and made a powerful appeal for the constitutional right of every citizen to choose for themselves their religion and method of treating disease.[1] This highly respected legislator's speech single-handedly shifted the momentum of the room, and when he finished, an appreciative group of Christian Scientists who were observing the proceedings approached to thank him.

Allen J. Greer. Photograph, courtesy of Minnesota Historical Society.

But where, he asked, might he find a Mrs. Thompson of Minneapolis? "She is the one I wish to speak to," he told them.

Greer walked over, greeted the quiet Christian Science practitioner who had been standing by herself watching the legislative session from the side of the room, and then explained to her what he had just done.

View of St. Paul, Minnesota, showing the State Capitol, circa 1890. Photograph, courtesy of Minnesota Historical Society.

"Mrs. Thompson, when I left my home this morning my little grandson called me back from the door and said, 'Grandpa, please save my Mrs. Thompson tonight,'" Greer said. "You will remember the little boy ... you saved [him] after the physicians had given him up as a hopeless case of heart trouble and asthma.

"Last evening he heard his mother questioning me at the dinner table about this medical bill, and I want you to know that this is one way of expressing my gratitude to you for the great healing you have brought into my home through Christian Science."[2]

The following day the proposed bill was voted down to defeat, the argument that carried the day coming from the mouth of a little boy testifying to Emma Thompson's healing work — the seed within itself bearing fruit after its kind.

The seed within itself

Some years previous as the train from Boston took her home to Minneapolis, one can imagine Emma Thompson sitting in her seat, perhaps a book on her lap, quietly looking out the window at the early autumn countryside with its splashes of gold and orange leaves.

Doubtless her thought turned back to a few days earlier when, sitting in Mary Baker Eddy's Primary class,[3] her heart burned within her as she drank in the things of the Spirit — of God's allness and goodness and of man's spiritual perfection as His image. Here were the things she had spent a lifetime searching for.

Now, as the train steamed westward, she may very well have thought to the days that lay ahead. The seed of Christian Science was to be planted into the frontier soil of Minnesota and she was being asked to play a crucial role in this work.

Perhaps questions rumbled up from the clickety-clack rhythm of the train on the tracks:

Could she do this?
Did she know enough?
Would she prove worthy?

After all, hadn't she wanted to flee Mrs. Eddy's class a few weeks earlier and return home after an attack of self-doubt, telling her teacher she felt she could not "honor" the Massachusetts Metaphysical College, only to be brought back by Mrs. Eddy's encouraging words?[4]

But living each day "faithful over a few things" had indeed brought her safely thus far in life — from a New England childhood struggling with a painful disease, to marriage, the birth of two daughters, and now, finally, to healing and the beginnings of spiritual transformation. But soon she would be back in Minnesota, twelve hundred miles from her teacher, to carry on this holy work alone.

Had Mrs. Thompson been able to peek into her future, she would see her gentle nature, soldier's loyalty, and CEO's work ethic gain in spiritual dominion and power. She would see patients come to her for healing from all over the United States. She would see herself literally ordering the dumb to speak, the blind to see, and the lame to walk. And she would see them obey.

Yet, that day on the train, she could not have known any of this any more than she could have known, when she healed Senator Greer's grandson, that one day it would help nudge a state legislature into an about-face on a bill.

Massachusetts Metaphysical College, located first (May 1882) at 569 Columbus Avenue, Boston, and moved to 571 in March 1884. Photograph, Longyear Museum Collection.

Indeed, here was the genius of living each day "faithful over a few things." It allowed one to be made "ruler over many."

One can almost imagine a smile on Mrs. Eddy's face after opening up one of Mrs. Thompson's earnest first letters and reading, there was "no obstacle I can't surmount."[5]

The obstacle that had driven Mrs. Thompson to Christian Science was a painful condition that had been medically diagnosed as neuralgia of the head, from which she had suffered since a young girl.

Emma Morgan was born in 1842 on a farm a few miles from Portland, Maine. The painful neuralgia rendered her "nearly frantic" at times according to her daughter Abigail Dyer Thompson and it kept her on a continual quest to find healing.[6]

Emma's hard work and drive for academic excellence resulted in her graduation with honors from North Yarmouth Academy in Yarmouth, Maine, and Waterville Academy in Waterville, Maine.

Colby College?

Early in her twenties, the attacks of neuralgia reached a point where traditional medicine offered no solution and she sought help from an unorthodox magnetic doctor, Phineas P. Quimby, in nearby Portland, Maine. It was here, in 1862, that she met another Quimby patient, Mary Patterson, later known as Mary Baker Eddy (see pages 32–34). But Quimby's treatment brought Emma no lasting relief, and she struggled on as best she could.

She became a schoolteacher, married, and moved to Minneapolis. Some years after their arrival, however, her husband passed away, leaving her alone to raise their two daughters, Abigail and Ella.

In 1884, now in her early forties and still seeking healing, Mrs. Thompson was given a copy of Mary Baker Eddy's work *Science and Health with Key to the Scriptures*. Abigail Thompson recounts how her mother studied the book night and day:

> The *earnest study of this book … brought a complete and permanent healing, and so illumined my mother's consciousness* that she was able to *bring the same remarkable freedom to a majority of those who turned to her for help.* Within a short time patients came to her in such large numbers that her days and nights were crowded with work.[7]

This healing proved the pivotal event in her life. Two years later she sat in the first of three classes with Mrs. Eddy at the Massachusetts Metaphysical College.[8]

Mrs. Thompson once told Calvin Frye, however, that her estimate of Mrs. Eddy was fixed even before she entered the classroom: "My own opinion was formed of my very dear Teacher when I read S[cience] & H[ealth]," she wrote Frye in 1888, "and nothing could change it."[9]

"The patients … began to come"

BY THE LATE 1880S, WORD HAD SPREAD THROUGHOUT MINNEAPOLIS OF THE extraordinary healings taking place downtown in the Victorian clapboard at 314 Sixth Street, South. What's more, the kindly lady with the thick braids and warm smile was said to follow Jesus' admonition, "Freely ye have received, freely give." She offered Christian Science treatment free of charge on Sundays.

One area resident reported the waiting line of patients sometimes filled the home's downstairs rooms. One morning Mrs. Thompson walked out from her "treating" room, saw her downstairs filled with patients and announced: "I cannot tell how long it will take to treat you all, but I will work as long as you will stay."[10] She made this announcement early in the day. The last patient left at three the next morning. *dedication*

Only a few weeks back from her Primary class in Boston and her practice was already flourishing. With her freshly-minted practitioner card appearing in that month's *Christian Science Journal*,[11] her full-time practice was officially under way. She dashed off a quick letter to her teacher as an early progress report:

> *Your teachings bring all of these truths so clear to me that I cannot see how any one by strictly following you can any way fail of success. Before I had eaten my breakfast — the patients ... began to come....*[12]

There were patients such as twenty-year-old Viola Horne, who came to see Mrs. Thompson after a doctor's examination revealed breast cancer. Told she had but a few months to live, she took the recommendation of an acquaintance whom Mrs. Thompson had healed of tuberculosis in its last stages, and went to see for herself.

On the third day of treatment, Mrs. Thompson said to her: "Now, dear, when you go away today, just leave this with me, as it does not belong to you."[13] A block away from the house, Viola knew she had been healed.

Her sister wrote that Viola returned "bouncing into our home exclaiming that she was healed and when mother asked her how she knew, she said, 'Oh, I just know it, Mother, I feel free!'"[14]

A second examination by the same doctor who had diagnosed the disease confirmed the healing.

There was Lena Steuerwald's brother, whom doctors had diagnosed with a stomach tumor. Mrs. Steuerwald reported that her father took her then eighteen-year-old brother to see a medical specialist in Minneapolis, but he was not helped.

After hearing about the new healer, the father brought his son to Emma Thompson's home. She gave him one treatment and he returned at about dinnertime to the boardinghouse where they were staying. For the previous three years he had been wasting away eating one-half cup of Mellon's baby food each day, and even that created excruciating pain.

"My brother said he felt hungry, and remembering that Mrs. Thompson had told him to eat whatever he wanted, he sat down to the table and ate an egg, two hot biscuits, some sauce, and drank a glass of milk," Mrs. Steuerwald wrote.[15] That night he fell into a sound sleep. The next morning he ate a hearty breakfast.

The complete healing came with a few additional treatments, and by the time the family returned to their Neillsville, Wisconsin, home two weeks later, the boy was completely healed. His sister reported that he became the heartiest and strongest member of the family — "the picture of health."

There was Mary E. Evans, who for many years had been unable to walk or use her arms. She came to see Mrs. Thompson and was healed in one visit. Her daughter, Grace De Vaux, included in her write-up of her mother's healing that she, too, had been healed by Mrs. Thompson that day of deafness and a nervous twitch.[16]

There was May E. Bullock, who came to the Thompson home in 1888 in utter hopelessness after doctors had diagnosed her with cancer. She had endured three unsuccessful operations and was told she had three months to live. At her first meeting with Mrs. Thompson, as she wrote in her terse testimonial, freedom came immediately:

> Was taken to Mrs. Thompson and the first treatment, was almost wholly relieved from pain. Strength returned. Could eat sleep well. In all had eight treatments.[17]

Written a decade after the healing, her testimonial confirmed that the disease never returned.

Uncompromising compassion

MRS. THOMPSON HELD A DEEP COMPASSION FOR HER PATIENTS. BUT FROM THE very beginning of her practice, she was uncompromising with any underlying error. Patients sometimes came to the Thompson house for healing while still clinging to what the medical community had defined as necessary.

Sometimes, when Mrs. Thompson detected a patient subtly leaning on such a false support — be it bandages, a medical support brace, crutches, or eyeglasses — she gently demanded to let it go. She felt that spiritual healing alone was the only true pity, the only real help. Sympathy for the disease subtly enforced the slavery.

Loren Chowen came to Mrs. Thompson for healing with eyes heavily bandaged, having spent a decade suffering from inflamed granulated eyelids. Chowen had been unable to see for three months previous to the visit.

"She had me remove the bandage as soon as I entered her presence," Chowen wrote in a testimony published in the January 1889 *Journal*. "After she gave me a treatment she requested me to open my eyes. I did, and was

Emma Thompson with unidentified child, circa 1890. Photograph, Longyear Museum Collection.

astonished to find the weakness gone. The light had no disagreeable effect upon them.... I felt that I had indeed experienced one of the miracles the Scriptures speak of."[18]

Mrs. Eugene Merrill had consulted leading medical specialists of Europe about an intense pain from an internal organic difficulty — what they called lack of a strong constitution. Doctors could not find a remedy.

One doctor had told her simply: "You could not expect a physician to furnish you with a constitution, now would you?"[19]

Mrs. Merrill had worn a brace for internal support for many years when she walked into the Thompson home to give this Christian Science religion a try. After she sat down she promptly announced to Mrs. Thompson that she didn't want to hear anything about the teachings of Christian Science. It was, she firmly believed, blasphemous.

Mrs. Merrill reported that every time she asked a question, her practitioner gently answered with a verse from the Bible, a book Mrs. Merrill had once loved but had now lost all faith in, calling its promises a "mockery."

"I do not see why you should not get well," Mrs. Thompson told her. "God is your life, and in Him you live, and move, and have your being."

Mrs. Merrill recalled that she began to feel better immediately. Mrs. Thompson then asked her to set aside the brace the doctors had given her to wear. She describes in her testimony how Mrs. Thompson asked her in a "low steady" voice:

> You have done everything the physicians have requested you to do, and they have told you they can do nothing more for you, so would it not be fair for you to do as you are asked now?[20]

Reasonable enough, Mrs. Merrill thought. She took the brace off and said she encountered great pain for thirty-six hours. Then it vanished and she knew she had been healed. Her testimony reports this healing was permanent.

The following summer, while pregnant with her fourth child, Mrs. Merrill wrote Mrs. Thompson for help, this time to address the nausea — the same condition that had attended her three earlier pregnancies:

> *I knew with perfect certainty the day [Mrs. Thompson]*
> *received my [letter], for the nausea and trembling ceased and*
> *I was entirely free for the remainder of the period.*[21]

Mrs. Merrill added that the birth took place with little pain. She also said that her family experienced many healings over forty years, some the direct result of Mrs. Thompson's work.

"Sometimes it seemed to me the most wonderful part was her never failing patience," Mrs. Merrill wrote. "Such a friend I have never known — so wise in counsel, and so steadfast in the knowledge of God."

Mrs. Merrill said that Mrs. Thompson's healing work was quick. On one occasion, after a doctor had diagnosed her son as having diphtheria, Mrs. Thompson was called onto the case later that same day. The next morning, when the doctor returned, he found the boy completely healed.

"Nothing that I have done for him has wrought the marvelous thing evident in this child since yesterday," the doctor told the boy's mother. "You had a bad-looking case here and now he is perfectly well. It is a higher power than mine that has done this work."

In the mid-1880s Lissette Getz was carried into the Thompson house with a knee fracture from a fall two years earlier that had left her an invalid.[22] Suffering what she described as "unendurable" pain, she used crutches for support.

> *After the first treatment [Mrs. Thompson] took away my*
> *crutches, and commanded me to walk. I improved very*
> *rapidly, and in two weeks I was able to walk seven blocks.*[23]

In her testimony, addressed to Mrs. Eddy and printed in the March 1888 *Journal*, Mrs. Getz reported that later that summer she had walked distances of five to six miles. Her healing also included release from long-standing chronic bronchitis, liver and stomach trouble, and nervous headache.

So grateful was Mrs. Getz for this healing that she took up the study of Christian Science. A short while later she suffered an inexplicable mental breakdown. Her family committed her to a mental institution, blaming the mental derangement on her study of *Science and Health*.

Mrs. Thompson went to the asylum to see her patient but was turned away at the entrance. She came home and wrote Mrs. Eddy of the particulars of the case and the claim of mental derangement.

Mrs. Eddy's quick reply instructed her how to handle the case:

> *The woman was not hurt reading truth — if error says that, it lies, and you know it, and you must establish the truth in your own and your patient's mind. You know there is but one Mind and there is no other to be deranged. There is no deranged mind — know this and make it appear.*[24]

When Mrs. Eddy's letter arrived, Mrs. Getz was instantly healed and released, as Mrs. Thompson reported in a letter to Mrs. Eddy. On the front of the envelope that held Mrs. Thompson's letter, Mrs. Eddy wrote: "Certif. of my healing."[25]

Mrs. Getz went to work for Mrs. Thompson as an assistant and eventually entered into the practice of Christian Science healing herself.

Adelaide M. Kinnear felt that eyeglasses were a necessity. By the time she came to the Thompson home for healing, she had failed to find relief from many difficulties that included weak eyes, stomach trouble, and indigestion. She had not eaten any substantial food for many months and drank only hot water and milk.

After her first treatment, Mrs. Kinnear asked her practitioner what she should eat and was told, "Anything that other people eat." She went out and had a hearty meal that included cucumbers, corn, and blackberries and reported no difficulty.

One day Mrs. Thompson told her it was time to lay aside her eyeglasses:

"When Jesus healed the blind, he didn't give glasses; glasses are a human invention."[26]

"Day by day she led me on," Mrs. Kinnear wrote, "so gently and yet so firmly, until I caught sight of that fresh universe of Life, Truth, and Love." It took twenty-seven treatments in all, but then "came the realization of the Truth, the meaning of the words, 'Sickness never was;' and with the vision so divinely clear came the physical freedom."[27]

"Go with him twain"

SOME CASES REQUIRED A LITTLE MORE PRACTICAL ATTENTION, AND MRS. Thompson was always willing to go the extra mile.

Despite her extraordinarily busy days in 1888 — "I now work from 7 a.m. to 10 p.m. hardly time to get my meals," she wrote Mrs. Eddy that year[28] — she still found time to leave her house and busy practice and go to a patient who had an urgent need. Called to the home of a Minneapolis police officer on a cold winter morning that year, Mrs. Thompson found the man unconscious from diphtheria, and a baby convulsed with a spasm.

Emma Thompson, *front row, left,* circa 1897.
Photograph, Longyear Museum Collection.

Treating them one at a time, she first took the baby from its mother, prayed, and handed it back, saying, "The baby will never have such again." And, according to the officer's daughter, Laura Fox, "she didn't."[29]

Mrs. Thompson then addressed the police officer, just returned to consciousness, and ordered him to throw up the medicines he had taken. He did. She stayed with him a few hours until he showed improvement.

A few days later, when his police supervisors ordered him back to work after learning that he was relying on Christian Science and not on medicine, off he went on patrol in the middle of winter.

Mrs. Thompson joined him, walking his police beat alongside him, all the while affirming the truth. The officer was healed. Eventually, all three of the policeman's daughters became devoted, class-taught Christian Scientists, and Laura became a *Journal*-listed Christian Science practitioner at the age of twenty-seven.

"Don't let the work worry you"

BY 1888 PATIENTS WERE COMING FROM ALL OVER THE UNITED STATES — a success Mrs. Thompson attributed to the fact that she did not deviate one iota from Mrs. Eddy's teaching. She wrote her teacher that autumn:

> *My success comes from strictly following to the best of my ability your teaching... never allowing it to be mixed with any one else.*[30]

We get something of a snapshot of Mrs. Thompson's approach to the practice of Christian Science healing from a letter she sent to encourage a young practitioner just getting started in the work. This practitioner had agreed to fill in for her so she could travel to New England to visit Mrs. Eddy.[31]

Mrs. Thompson wrote this directive on healing after having spent some time with Mrs. Eddy and, no doubt, it reflects some of what the two had talked about:

> *Don't let the work worry you. Only do the best you can, and*
> *don't for one moment hold the thought that anyone is sick*
> *and then expect to see them get well. There is no disease —*
> *then you have none to heal. Hold always the perfect, which*
> *means all are perfect in God, for God is All. In that way and*
> *no other can we lose all personality.*[32]

Mrs. Thompson, then in her sixth year of practice, also encouraged this practitioner to deal with the ups and downs of daily practice as simply another element to be addressed in the work and placed under God's care:

> *And if some days seem a little more cloudy than others,*
> *remember this is a human belief too, and handle it as all*
> *other beliefs or thoughts by placing the perfect thought in*
> *consciousness that brings us nearer to God....*
>
> *Our Savior did not ask those who turned to him if they felt*
> *better, but declared to them the Truth, and then commanded*
> *them to demonstrate it themselves, by walking, seeing, hear-*
> *ing, all in realization, and so must we.*[33]

"So must we"

ASK A ROOMFUL OF *FORTUNE* 500 CHIEF EXECUTIVES HOW THEY GO ABOUT achieving success and you'll probably hear the buzzwords: vision, plan, daily goals, hard work, and focus, focus, focus.

While Mrs. Thompson defined success quite differently from the business world, her determination to become a scientific healer expressed itself in a laserlike focus on her mission. This daily focus, combined with an extraordinary work ethic, would be the envy of any corporate boardroom today.

Mrs. Eddy recognized the need for such single-mindedness and concentrated effort from her own experience in the healing work, writing to a student:

> *I know that a healer needs all her time to do her best in car-*
> *ing for the patients. It is an absorbing subject to lift the mind*
> *above pain, disease, and death and when I practiced I could*
> *not attend to aught else.*[34]

Mrs. Eddy quietly took note of Mrs. Thompson's devotion to this goal of becoming a scientific healer and mentioned it to Mrs. Thompson's daughter Abigail during one of the young woman's periodic visits to Pleasant View in the autumn of 1896:

> *As a rule my students have wanted to heal, and preach, and*
> *teach,… In contrast to this, your mother has been satisfied to*
> *do just this one thing — to heal the sick — and she has been*
> *humble enough, and selfless enough to continue steadfast in*
> *the healing work until she has given to the world an exact*
> *proof of the way Christian Science should be demonstrated.*[35]

During this visit Mrs. Eddy requested Abigail to keep a record of her healing work. "You should, dear, be faithful in keeping an exact record of your demonstrations," Mrs. Eddy instructed, "for you never know when they might prove valuable to the Cause in meeting attacks on Christian Science."[36] Both mother and daughter complied and their personal papers and corre-spondence preserved at Longyear Museum include a separate file of their healing testimonials.

"I like originality … I love honesty"

AN ESSENTIAL INGREDIENT IN MRS. THOMPSON'S SUCCESS WAS THE COMPLETE honesty she brought to the healing work. Whispering pride or self-justification might tempt some to hide their weaknesses or failures in order to save face. Mrs. Thompson, however, would have none of it.

"I shall expect you to chide me and censor me as you see fit," she wrote Mrs. Eddy early on, "and any advice will be most cordially received now. I have many faults, and I want you to watch me closely."[37]

Here was an ethic of honesty and a willingness to learn all things rightly and then to give the glory to God when healing occurred — a lesson one of Mrs. Thompson's patients learned firsthand.

After being healed of dumbness that had lasted ten years, Nancy Hudec went to thank her practitioner for the wonderful healing. Mrs. Thompson let her know, as Nancy Hudec recounted in her testimony, who should receive her gratitude:

> [*Mrs. Thompson*] *tells me I must not thank her, but look to God, as it is through Him the blind are made to see and the dumb to speak.*[38]

Complete and permanent healing was Mrs. Thompson's only standard. She had witnessed this twice when Mrs. Eddy instantaneously healed her daughter Abigail from life-threatening situations.

The first healing was in 1886 after Abigail let out a deep cough, perhaps stemming from what she called three generations of family "lung trouble." Upon hearing this one day at the Massachusetts Metaphysical College, Mrs. Eddy realized the seriousness of the condition and gave Abigail a treatment. The cough stopped immediately and never returned.[39]

The second healing took place a year later after Abigail had suffered a severe hip injury. Notified that the case was turning serious, Mrs. Eddy stepped in and prayed. The result was another instantaneous cure.[40]

Mrs. Eddy's quick, complete healings formed the standard for Mrs. Thompson's own practice, and she accepted nothing less for her patients. In the 1887 Obstetrics class, in which Mrs. Thompson was a student, Mrs. Eddy commented on her student's high standard and ethical aspiration: "Mrs. Thompson," Mrs. Eddy said in front of the class, "you are original and I like originality; but more than all, you are honest and I love honesty."[41]

"Nothing before you but denial of self"

THE APOSTLE PAUL OPENS HIS LETTER TO THE ROMANS BY STATING HIS relationship to Christ: "Paul, a servant of Jesus Christ."[42] The Greek word rendered "servant" actually signifies *slave.* This sense goes to the very crux of Christian discipleship. While the human mind may recoil from such a term, seeing in it only bondage, Paul argues in this letter that, in fact, it is a slavery that holds the only real freedom.

Mrs. Eddy spoke in similar tones to the students in her 1889 Normal class, telling them that, while a student could come and sit in her Primary class and treat the experience as a kind of "transaction," she expected a very different level of commitment from her Normal class students:

> *When you come to this class I want you to feel that there is nothing before you but denial of self.*[43]

This "not my will, but Thine, be done" attitude is evident throughout Mrs. Thompson's spiritual transformation. It runs like a thread through her letters to Mrs. Eddy across nearly a quarter century. Like time-lapse photography, these letters reveal an unfolding devotion to her healing mission, to Christian Science, and to Mrs. Eddy. Each one — a snapshot of a particular moment — shows an extraordinary desire and willingness to place herself in God's service.

Combing through this correspondence, one finds stray comments — some small detail or circumstance — that reveal the cost she was willing to pay to establish herself as one of Minneapolis's first practitioners:

> *I have no time from early morning till late at night.*[44]

> *Hardly time for sleep.*[45]

> *I am now working fifteen hours per day not one moment to spare.*[46]

Indeed, one Sunday morning in 1903, very near the time for the start of the church service, Mrs. Thompson found herself face to face with a husband pleading for help for his severely ill wife. Mrs. Leonard from Waverly, Minnesota, had long suffered from the effects of a powerful drug given by a doctor. Instead of healing her, the prescription had burned her stomach lining.

With the church hour approaching, Mrs. Thompson thought it would be better to attend the service first and see the patient later in the day. But the husband pleaded, and Mrs. Thompson took the woman into the treatment room.

Sitting in the waiting room while his wife was with Mrs. Thompson, Mr. Leonard looked up a few minutes later to see his wife walk through the door:

> There was such freedom and light in [his wife's] face that he
> felt immediately she had been healed.

That was the only treatment given to her, and the healing remained permanent. She continued in good health for thirty years — always giving the credit to Christian Science for her remarkable recovery.[47]

The seed of healing, the blossom of church

CHRISTIAN SCIENCE TEACHER AND PRACTITIONER ANNIE M. KNOTT HAD once offered Mrs. Thompson's daughter Abigail an interesting metaphor to describe the formation of Christian Science churches. In the early years, many patients walked daily from practitioners' offices completely healed and then went on their merry way, never to be heard from again.

Mrs. Knott likened these people to polished beads that had rolled away. The church, Mrs. Knott told her friend, served as a piece of string that gathered the beads together, thus providing form and strength.[48]

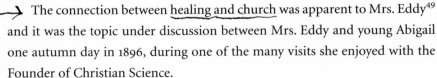 The connection between healing and church was apparent to Mrs. Eddy[49] and it was the topic under discussion between Mrs. Eddy and young Abigail one autumn day in 1896, during one of the many visits she enjoyed with the Founder of Christian Science.

Explaining her concept of organization, Mrs. Eddy emphasized the importance of "a strong foundation of healing before a Christian Science church should be started." Then she turned to Abigail and announced that she wanted her to relay a message to her mother:

> *I want you to take this word back to your mother, to organize a Second Church in Minneapolis, and tell her that the church she founds will stand, because it will be built on a solid foundation of Christian Science healing.* [50]

Soon after Abigail returned home, the work of founding another branch church in Minneapolis began. The sheer quantity of Mrs. Thompson's healing works had already taken care of the "beads" part of this equation. Indeed, those who had been healed were "rolling" all over Minneapolis. They lacked only the string to hold them together.

Construction of Second Church of Christ, Scientist, Eleventh Street and Second Avenue, Minneapolis, Minnesota, 1901.
Photograph, courtesy of Second Church of Christ, Scientist, Minneapolis.

Lyceum Theater, Hennepin Avenue between Seventh and Eighth streets, Minneapolis, Minnesota. Photograph, Sweet, courtesy of Minnesota Historical Society.

Examining the history and development of Second Church of Christ, Scientist, Minneapolis, is a little like watching one of those nature documentaries where a colorful spring flower bursts forth into blossom. Indeed, this single branch church rapidly unfolded and sent out shoots that resulted in three additional Minneapolis branches.

Organized by Emma Thompson, who was elected its first president, Second Church conducted its first service on February 7, 1897. It was attended by the forty-seven charter members and about two hundred other attendees, who huddled inside a little frame structure owned by the Swedenborgian Society. Adelaide Kinnear's testimony of her healing, related earlier, offers an eyewitness account of how quickly this church came together.

Mrs. Kinnear said she joined the newly created Second Church, Minneapolis, in July 1897 — roughly eight to ten months after Mrs. Eddy's request to Abigail that it be started. At that point, she said, the church contained 119 members.[51]

The following year, Mrs. Thompson wrote her teacher of the rich harvest under way in this church:

> *Our church in Minneapolis is growing rapidly and now*
> *although the youngest in Minnesota is larger than any two*
> *others put together in the state.*[52]

The church continued to grow rapidly. By June 1898 they had moved to a larger building and added a Sunday evening service. The following year a Reading Room was opened and mission services were started for the county jail, city workhouse, Home for Children and Aged Women, and Bethany House. That year the Sunday service, bursting at its seams, was again moved, to the large auditorium in the Lyceum Theater.

In 1901 more space was needed and so the midweek meeting was moved into the more spacious Unitarian Church.

The members of Second Church realized they needed their own edifice and on September 20, 1903, they held the dedicatory service of their new, large, purpose-built Gothic edifice located at Eleventh Street and Second Avenue. Over 5,000 people attended the 11:00 AM and 3:30 PM services.[53]

By 1908 it was necessary to divide the membership into two new churches: Fifth Church was created in March and Sixth Church in July. In 1915 Fourth Church was created to relieve the overcrowding still taking place in Second Church.[54] With expanding activities demanding more space, Second Church constructed new church facilities in the 1930s.

The fruitful history of this church and its offshoots, recorded by Abbie Stein, Clerk of Second Church in 1935, attributes the rapid growth to the work of Emma Thompson:

> *Second Church is the natural outgrowth of the healing work*
> *of Mrs. Emma A. Thompson, the pioneer Christian Scientist*
> *of the Northwest.*[55]

Mrs. Eddy herself sent a telegram on the occasion of the dedication of Second Church:

Second Church of Christ, Scientist, Eleventh Street and Second Avenue,
Minneapolis, Minnesota, 1903.
Photograph, courtesy of Second Church of Christ, Scientist, Minneapolis.

> Beloved: — *The spiritual dominates the temporal. Love*
> *gives nothing to take away. Nothing dethrones His house.*
> *You are dedicating yours to Him. Protesting against error,*
> *you unite with all who believe in Truth. God guard and*
> *guide you.*[56]

"Then appeared the tares also"

IN HIS PARABLE OF THE TARES AND WHEAT, JESUS REVEALED TO HIS DISCIPLES
how evil attempts to challenge good while seeming to grow right alongside
it. When the wheat appeared, Jesus told his students, "then appeared the
tares also."[57]

This seeming synchronicity of the tares becoming apparent *then* — at the
very same time as the wheat — seemed to be the order of events that unfolded

in Mrs. Thompson's life. But it also forced her to a higher level of Christian Science demonstration.

Many of Mrs. Thompson's letters to Mrs. Eddy contain a sentence or two reporting on the bountiful harvest of wheat she was experiencing — much success in healing:

> *Since I left Boston doubts — fears have vanished like dew before the sun. Yes, — God is all to me. He leadeth me.*[58]

> *Now in my fourth year sitting from early morn till late at night have arrived to the place I wanted namely the best Healer, not for fame, only to show the Truth — as Mrs. Eddy teaches — was the truth. And now my work must talk for me....*[59]

> *Since my return [from visiting you] one year ago this month I have gained more understanding than all the seven years of work, seven this fall.*[60]

> *The interest that is taken in Science with us is certainly wonderful. I have never seen anything like it.*[61]

But with this abundant harvest of wheat came periods of gathering and burning tares. In Mrs. Thompson's life this translated into periods of severe wrestling with a variety of challenges — the local medical community, the Minneapolis faction of mind-curers, other local churches, and the press.

Many of Mrs. Thompson's healings had overruled some local doctor's death sentence on a patient, and as word of these decisive demonstrations of the power of Christian Science got around town, it had the effect of setting off a bomb in a beehive.

Buzzing was fully evident from a Sunday feature article that appeared in the *Minneapolis Tribune* on September 25, 1887, on the subject of Christian Science in Minneapolis. It was followed on September 30, 1887, by a large "letters to the editor" column in which readers offered their opinions of the new faith.

Minneapolis doctor Edward J. Brown, M.D., wrote to ask that something be done to protect Minneapolis's citizens from Christian Science. His letter asked the local clergy to rise up and join the fray:

> *During the two years past in which the Christian Science fanaticism has raged so extensively, almost nothing has been done so far as the general public are aware, by the clergy of this city, to guard the people against its pervasive influence.*[62]

The lively response of letters to the original article drew a second batch a few days later. This group included a commentator who equated Christian Science with the "mind-cure movement" in Minneapolis: "The 'mind cure' or 'imagination cure' is not necessarily rendered a sacred thing by being carried on in the name of religion," wrote this unnamed commentator, who went on to inform readers that the next meeting of the local Presbyterian Alliance would consider the hot topic of Christian Science in Minneapolis.

These press attacks had the effect of placing Mrs. Thompson under the klieg lights for all to see. After all, she was the city's best-known practitioner of Christian Science, who had been taught by its Founder, Mary Baker Eddy, and a single failure now — especially if it involved a child — would be delightful grist for her enemies to grind up and feed to the hungry front pages of local newspapers.

So the stakes were raised one summer night when Mrs. Thompson received a father's urgent call for help. His little girl was suffering from scarlet fever, a case the local family doctor had described as near death. Mrs. Thompson arrived at the man's home just about midnight and prayed for about an hour. She then returned home, leaving the child sleeping peacefully.

Returning the next morning, the family doctor discovered the little girl sitting up in bed playing with her toys after having eaten a hearty breakfast. When he found out that a Christian Science practitioner had healed her, he grew angry and placed a quarantine sign on the front of the house, telling the family, "I am leaving on a fishing trip and I would like to see Mrs. Thompson get you out of quarantine."

Emma Thompson. Photograph, courtesy of
Second Church of Christ, Scientist, Minneapolis.

When a member of the family contacted Mrs. Thompson later that day about the sign, Mrs. Thompson said to her, "The same power that healed your child can remove the sign from your house."

That evening, in a decisive turn of events, a severe windstorm destroyed the sign, scattering it throughout the neighborhood.[63]

"Oh, what an enemy is envy"

THE CUMULATIVE EFFECT OF THE MANY ATTACKS ON CHRISTIAN SCIENCE during its early years in Minneapolis sometimes turned Mrs. Thompson's path into a steep climb. Not wanting to burden Mrs. Eddy with all the details, Mrs. Thompson's letters only hint at the challenge she was meeting. Sometimes a single sentence rings out like a plaintive cry registering the weight she felt on her shoulders:

> *Have had some very aggravating things to contend with —*
> *oh, what an enemy is envy.*[64]

The envy in this case came from a small, mostly local group of spiritual "questers" who had entered the doors of the burgeoning Christian Science movement, only to exit and join one of the then-trendy strains of mind-cure. But not before making a concerted effort to draw Mrs. Thompson away with them. First they tried to convince her that Mrs. Eddy was not the originator of Christian Science. They invited her to come take healing instruction with one of their teachers. They then accused her of idolizing Mrs. Eddy. When none of that worked, they went after her patients.

In a letter dated January 13, 1889, she informed Mrs. Eddy of what she called a "considerable disturbance" gathering force in Minneapolis. "I meet with so much envy here and it seems about every disloyal student comes here," Mrs. Thompson wrote, listing the various Christian Scientists who had turned to mind-cure and who were a part of the Minneapolis scene.

A widow raising two daughters alone, holding down a home with almost every moment of a day accounted for, and busy with her large daily practice, Mrs. Thompson now had to make time to thrust and parry with this enemy.

Sometimes it proved to be a baptism by fire. Indeed, her earliest battles with two mind-curers — a Mrs. Root and a Mrs. Merrick — involved colossal mental wrestlings that sent her into a tailspin.

Mrs. Thompson, barely a month out of the Primary class, sent Mrs. Eddy a frantic call for help: "I've lost my bearings," she wrote on October 25, 1886.

> *I was never in all my life in a condition like the present. And*
> *how did I get here? I am in a terrible numb state. I can't*
> *treat, I can't think and to think of you is impossible.*[65]

Mrs. Eddy replied five days later. In a long letter she gently brought Mrs. Thompson through this trial and showed her how to address, point by point, what was really at work:

> *Your experience at this time is most promising, every one that stands by me and is governed by God, the Divine Principle of his work, will experience from the influence of Satan trying him, just what you do. It is only the influence of malicious mesmerism, the influence of a lie. Now remember dear, your cardinal points in Science viz that a lie is never true. Truth & Love are your only Life, Substance and Intelligence or Mind and you cannot lose your true Mind any more than God can.*[66]

In her letter Mrs. Eddy pointed to the growth and gratitude that would result from this experience:

> *But you are privileged to have this battle with the lie early in your labors, and why? Because God knows you are equal to meeting it and putting it down.... And you are enduring it, temptation, that is all, and are growing under it. You will come out of this ten thousand times as strong in Truth as you went into it. Just know there is no power, no spell in animal magnetism, no electricity, no brains, no nerves, and no intelligence or power in mortal mind, alias evil, — and that Truth, Good, is omnipotent, has all power and it governs you and all error, evil, is under your feet. See this, know it, and after forty days' and nights' experience, like the blessed Master, you will have angels minister to you, — white winged higher and holier views of divine Science and thank God for what you have learned.*

About five months later, after another severe battle with the mind-curers, Mrs. Thompson again sent her teacher another cry for help, to which Mrs. Eddy replied:

> You have nothing to fear from 10000 mind-curers. Why do
> you feel shocked at things unreal? There is no power in evil
> a million of ciphers make no number. Evil a naught; why do
> you call it a unit and units?[67]

Mrs. Eddy's letter helped bring Mrs. Thompson out of the tailspin. Like a kite lifted by an opposing wind, she rose above the challenge, and her letters never again mention a tailspin of this magnitude. Almost certainly referring to these events, she wrote Calvin Frye the following year:

> I wish ... you could only see where I have stood the enemy
> doing their best to destroy me, malice envy hatred met me on
> every side but truth was my shield and my Parent of Divine
> Wisdom gently and onward led me.[68]

Mrs. Thompson would later come to the conclusion that, as the Bible said, the wrath of man would praise God, and wrote to Mrs. Eddy, "The persecution seems the best advertising C.S. can have."[69]

The Quimby connection

PERHAPS IT HAD NEVER OCCURRED TO MRS. THOMPSON THAT THERE MIGHT be a connection between her struggles with the mind-curers in the 1880s and the fact that she had been a patient of the magnetic doctor in Maine, Phineas P. Quimby, over twenty years earlier.

And yet, Quimby's treatments of so long ago had apparently left open a mental door that needed closing. Mrs. Eddy made the connection quickly and, in the same letter in which she told her she had "nothing to fear from 10000 mind-curers," pointed this out to her:

> *Rise from this* nightmare *of mesmerism. Quimby left this*
> *stain on your mortal belief now wash it off in Science, Chris-*
> *tian Science that rests in calm strength on the sure foundation*
> *that* God is All *and whatever else seems to be,* contradict *and*
> know it is not.[70]

Addressing and removing the stain Quimby had left on her mortal belief lifted Mrs. Thompson above the struggle and proved to be another crucial step in her spiritual development. It became critical for her to make a clear distinction between Christian Science on the one hand, where God, divine Mind, is the only source of true thought, and the mind-cure cafeteria of theologies and mental systems of healing on the other.

The underlying issues here would be the difference between success and failure. Christian Science teaches that God is the only power, the only cause, and thus the only healer. Surrendering to God's will and goodness, as demonstrated by Christ Jesus, is reflected in Christian experience as healing and redemption.

In contrast, Quimby's system used the human mind and will in order to heal, thus attempting to appropriate divine power. Christian surrender to the will of God is antithetical to Quimbyism, in which the mind-curer's unchecked ego would influence and control the patient's mind.

Mrs. Eddy had already addressed this point about mind-cure in *The Christian Science Journal* a few years earlier, in 1885, after being asked if the theology of Christian Science aided its healing:

> *Without its theology there is no mental science, no order that*
> *proceeds from God. All Science is divine, not human, in ori-*
> *gin and demonstration. . . . Take away the theology of mental*
> *healing and you take away its science, leaving it a human*
> *"mind-cure," nothing more nor less, — even one human*
> *mind governing another; by which, if you agree that God is*
> *Mind, you admit that there is more than one government*
> *and God.*[71]

"I have waited long years for this testimony"

"MRS. EDDY HAS NOT CHANGED MUCH SINCE I SAW her last," Emma Thompson told Calvin Frye in August 1886.[72] She had just entered the Massachusetts Metaphysical College for Primary class instruction and the second day of class was about to begin.

Now in her early forties, Mrs. Thompson had come to Boston to be taught Christian Science by Mary Baker Eddy, the author of *Science and Health with Key to the Scriptures,* the book that had healed Mrs. Thompson of many years' illness and suffering.

Phineas P. Quimby, circa 1860. Photograph, Longyear Museum Collection.

On the first day of class, she recognized her teacher as none other than the Mrs. Daniel Patterson she had met in Portland, Maine, in 1862, when the two had been patients of Phineas Parkhurst Quimby.

When Mrs. Thompson was a young woman, she had suffered periodically from severe attacks of neuralgia of the head. After witnessing one of these attacks, her father summoned the "magnetic healer" from Portland, Maine.

Arriving at the Morgans' farm, Quimby was startled by the intensity of Emma's agony. The pain could be so great that she had often requested her somewhat rotund mother to please place a pillow over her (Emma's) head and then sit on the pillow. This was an attempt to counteract the internal pressure.

Quimby asked for a washbowl filled with water and then for family members to leave the room. Mrs. Thompson wrote in a 1907 affidavit, "He said he could not control my mind with anyone else present." She stated:

> *His treatment consisted in placing bands on his*
> *wrists, plunging his hands in cold water, manipu-*
> *lating the head and making passes down the body.*
> *He asked me to concentrate my mind on him and*
> *to think of nothing and nobody but him.*[73]

When Quimby treated patients, he mentally "took on" the patient's disease. After treating Emma, his own suffering became so severe that Emma's father, Pitman Morgan, had to assist him to a bed at the Morgan house. He spent the rest of that night mentally trying to rid himself of the disease he had "taken on."

By the next morning, Emma's condition had greatly improved. At breakfast her father got out his checkbook and offered the magnetic doctor $1,000 — a huge sum in the 1860s — if he would divulge the secret of how he was able to relieve, at least somewhat, the suffering.

"I cannot, I do not understand it myself," Quimby replied.

As Quimby was about to leave, Emma's mother asked him what they should do if another attack were to occur, to which Quimby replied, "Tell your daughter to put her mind on me, and drink all the water she can."

There were further attacks for which Emma would have to travel to Quimby's Portland office for treatment. On the first of these visits Quimby introduced her to a Mrs. Patterson. Little did Emma then know the profound influence this slender, elegant lady from New Hampshire would have on her life. Quimby told Emma, "This is a very wonderful woman, and in comparison I am the man, but Mary is the Christ."[74] Mrs. Eddy herself later recalled Quimby's making a similar comment, comparing himself to John the Baptist and her to Christ, which statement she considered blasphemous and for which she rebuked him:

*But afterwards I concluded that he only referred to
the coming anew of Truth, which we both desired;
for in some respects he was quite a seer and understood what I said better than some others did....
Had his remark related to my personality, I should
still think that it was profane.*[75]

Twenty-four years later, upon entering the classroom at the
Massachusetts Metaphysical College, Mrs. Thompson recognized that
her teacher was none other than the Mrs. Daniel Patterson whom
Quimby had introduced to her in 1862.

As the second day of teaching was about to begin, Mr. Frye went to
inform Mrs. Eddy of Mrs. Thompson's statement about their prior
acquaintance in Portland. Mrs. Eddy entered the classroom and asked
her to stand and relate to the class her experience with Quimby.

Mrs. Thompson described the attacks of neuralgia that had led
her to Quimby and then in 1884 to *Science and Health.* Only after reading *Science and Health,* she told the class, did the disease disappear for
good and she found herself permanently healed.

Mrs. Eddy replied, "I have waited long years for this testimony."

Mrs. Eddy later told her that she (Mrs. Thompson) had virtually
come to her rescue by making a clear firsthand statement about the
distinction between the hypnotic nature of Quimby's treatment and
the spiritual nature of Christian Science.

A brief statement containing these points was carried in the November 1886 *Journal.*[76] Years later, Mrs. Thompson would reproduce
this testimony in a detailed sworn affidavit, which she signed on February 23, 1907.

"That dear voice still rings"

THROUGHOUT HER LIFE, MRS. THOMPSON'S LOVE FOR HER TEACHER EXPRESSED itself in various ways, large and small. The sweet time she spent in Mrs. Eddy's classroom sometimes came back to her thought with great power, and as her busy days of caring for others flew by, she sometimes recalled herself sitting in her seat at the Massachusetts Metaphysical College, listening as her teacher illumined the truth of being.

"Now I read your book and that dear voice still rings 'All is Mind,'" Mrs. Thompson wrote Mrs. Eddy after an extremely intense period of struggle. "How much that means to me now. I love to live all those days I sat in your class over again. What struggles I can now appreciate; my lesson thru suffering has been a most valuable one for me."[77]

Such devotion to her teacher remained a constant all her life, and when she discovered Mrs. Eddy needing something she could supply, she would respond quickly and generously.

In December 1887, after learning that Mrs. Eddy was furnishing her new Boston home at 385 Commonwealth Avenue, Mrs. Thompson sent a $1,000 check — a small fortune in those days. Mrs. Eddy had not requested anything from her, but the money was sent quietly with no fanfare. This took place a little over a year after her first class with Mrs. Eddy.

To show her affection, Mrs. Thompson sent her teacher a brooch in the form of a crown with pearls. Mrs. Eddy's December 1892 letter of thanks included this appreciation of her student:

> I feel just this — that you are an honor to me and I would lay a crown on your head if it signified my desire to honor you and befitted poor mortals.[78]

Commenting that she had long worn a "crown of thorns," Mrs. Eddy called her the "first one to rebuke the cross with a crown. Precious Child, you are right, all is loyal, grand and enthroned that belongs to Christian Science."

Christian Science Hall, Concord, New Hampshire.
Photograph, H. L. Dunbar, C.S.B., 1898, Longyear Museum Collection.

And Mrs. Thompson was one of the first contributors of $1,000 to Mrs. Eddy's appeal to a select number of her students for The Mother Church building fund, prompting another letter of thanks from her teacher:

> *Now dear one, it is pleasant for me to think of having your name with mine in the silent safe recess of a rock;[79] and still pleasanter to think of our being rising together till we rest in the realm of eternal harmony.*
>
> *Where no arrow wounds the dove,*
> *Where no partings are for love.[80]*

Mrs. Eddy's statement that each donation for this church "came promptly; sometimes at much self-sacrifice"[81] was certainly true in Mrs. Thompson's case:

the thousand dollars she sent was money she had carefully set aside to pay an upcoming tax bill.

But her daughter Abigail reported that after sending the money to Mrs. Eddy, funds poured into the Thompson home from "unexpected sources," and her mother was able to pay her taxes on time.[82]

"The Chariot of clouds"

FROM ATOP THE PLATFORM OF CHRISTIAN SCIENCE HALL IN CONCORD, NEW Hampshire, Mrs. Eddy addressed the students in her last class — the class of 1898. When she came to Emma Thompson, Mrs. Eddy stopped and commended this most loyal student and trusted friend: "I recognize you, student, as one who has worked long and faithfully in the vineyard."[83]

A simple tribute to this worker whose single focus was to live Christian Science and prove that, as she once told Calvin Frye, "earnestness and firmness conquers every foe."[84]

A fellow student in the classroom that day recorded the gratitude the sixty-six other students felt on hearing Mrs. Eddy pay tribute to Mrs. Thompson: "Everyone present was thankful that this devoted student received this mark of deep appreciation from the Discoverer of Christian Science," Daisette McKenzie wrote in her reminiscence. "The beautiful healing work which she had done was well known and deeply appreciated by the field."[85]

What it cost Mrs. Thompson personally to reach the level of achievement she attained in healing, and the countless times she silently stood as a strong voice for Christian Science in Minneapolis against the hostility and antagonism of the day, is the part of this story that is fully known only to her. We catch only small glimpses through the windows of her words.

But it is a fact that by the time she passed on December 24, 1913, Mrs. Thompson had tended the Minneapolis vineyard for just under thirty years. One can extrapolate from what is known about her practice and healing work, that the healings and spiritual transformations she brought about could very well have numbered in the thousands.

Many of those healings began with a simple visit to the sweet, caring lady who answered the door at 314 Sixth Street, South, in downtown Minneapolis with a smile.

Mrs. Thompson once wrote Calvin Frye: "I would sooner be a doorkeeper for Mrs. Eddy than occupy the finest mansion in Boston."[86]

But Mrs. Eddy saw something much finer for her dear friend:

> *And may you be a Mother in Israel following meekly as I have trod the footsteps of the flock. And as time rolls on and I advance to new demonstrations and can give higher lessons in the reflection of my own life, Oh may you be* by my side *in the race, in the Chariot of clouds.*[87]

Abigail Dyer Thompson

Preparation of
a Practitioner

Abigail Dyer Thompson, C.S.B., circa 1898.
Photograph, Longyear Museum Collection.

ABIGAIL DYER THOMPSON
PREPARATION OF A PRACTITIONER

AS SHE MOVED DOWN THE RECEPTION LINE TOWARD HER TEACHER, ABIGAIL Dyer Thompson prepared how she would thank Mary Baker Eddy for what she had just received.

The November 1898 class had just ended and this smart looking woman of about twenty — one of the youngest of the group of nearly seventy — stood out like a bright spring flower.

Mrs. Eddy had selected the names for this Normal class with great care, calling together not only the pillars of the current movement — the professorial likes of Edward A. Kimball and Judge Septimus J. Hanna — but also a contingent of the up-and-coming generation who were fast making their way into the vineyard and taking up work alongside their elders.

As she often did at the beginning of a class, Mrs. Eddy had gone around the room addressing students and, arriving at Abigail's mother, Emma Thompson, singled her out for her years of faithful service in the vineyard — extraordinary healing work that had become the talk of Minneapolis and that over the next decade would result in a remarkable increase in the number of churches there.

But the next chapter of the Christian Science story was already being written. Indeed, in a mere thirteen months from this class, calendars would flip to the new year 1900 and from this threshold one could see the clutch of progress being let out on the twentieth century, sending incredible power to the wheels of American invention and industry.

In the new century, Christian Science would encounter both remarkable growth and startling resistance. With this in mind, Mrs. Eddy saw this, her last class, as, in part, an invitation — calling new names to step forward to meet a new century's challenges.

Miss Abigail Dyer Thompson was one of those names.

Finally reaching her teacher, she shook Mrs. Eddy's hand. She had decided that words were not up to the job of expressing her gratitude and so, in effect, she offered her teacher a promise: "I have no words to express my gratitude for the great inspiration you have given me, but I hope my life may."

Mrs. Eddy placed her hand over her student's, looked into her eyes and said: "It will dear, it will."[1]

"The genius of progress is really the genius of work"

WALKING OUT OF CHRISTIAN SCIENCE HALL INTO THE STREETS OF CONCORD that day after the final class ended, Miss Thompson was determined to turn her final few words to Mrs. Eddy that day into a reality.

Indeed, in the account she wrote of what had transpired in the 1898 class, her last sentence shows the compass course she had already set for herself:

> My greatest desire since that memorable day has been that some time my healing work may prove worthy of her inspired teaching.[2]

How Miss Thompson brought that desire to fruition, taking her place alongside her mother as a noted Christian Science practitioner, is a story of dedication and love — love for God, for Christian Science, and for its Leader.

It is also a story of how focus, persistence, and hard work manifest an ideal, in this case a spiritual ideal, which would transform a young woman into a Christian Science practitioner whose service spanned the first half of the twentieth century to her passing in 1957.

"The genius of progress is really the genius of work," Miss Thompson said to fellow members of Second Church of Christ, Scientist, Minneapolis, in 1933,

Christian Science Hall, Concord, New Hampshire.
Photograph, W. G. C. Kimball, circa 1900, Longyear Museum Collection.

"the ability to see a goal and move steadily towards it without wavering, in the spirit of Paul when he said, 'this one thing I do' (Phil 3:13)."[3]

It was this single focus that led her, step by step, to the spiritual dominion that resulted in healing countless cases of disease, including "last hope" cases diagnosed by doctors as "incurable," among them a man told by doctors that his appendix had ruptured and they could do no more for him; an eleven-year-old with a heart condition beyond the scope of medicine; a man facing lifelong invalidism from a severe accident.

Obedience — The shaping of the rosebush

FOR MISS THOMPSON, WHO WOULD COUNT MARY BAKER EDDY AS A GOOD friend, learning life's spiritual lessons through obedience began early on.

Growing up under the shadow of her mother — one of Minneapolis's pre-eminent Christian Science practitioners — Miss Thompson had to learn *for herself* the answers to life's great questions: What is the nature of God? How are one's ideals manifested? How is healing accomplished?

These were subjects foremost in the thought of Mary Baker Eddy, and Miss Thompson's instruction from the Discoverer and Founder of Christian Science began on a September day in 1886, when Abigail, about eight years old, and her sister, Ella, found themselves alone with Mrs. Eddy in a small classroom of their own.

Their mother was currently a student in Mrs. Eddy's Primary class at the Massachusetts Metaphysical College. Between sessions Mrs. Eddy saw the little girls and held another little "class." The secret to mastery in life, Mrs. Eddy told her little students, was in the way a gardener trains a rosebush. He takes the young plant, Mrs. Eddy showed the two girls, and begins bending its branches in the direction he wants them to grow. Over time the bush begins to take on the symmetry and beauty that the gardener's ideal has set for it.

Abigail took this lesson to heart. Decades later she would write: "From this simile [Mrs. Eddy] drew the...lesson that every child should hold a clear standard of living that would finally mold thought and action into an ideal character."[4]

Like a rosebush being shaped into greater beauty and strength, Abigail was early trained into a life of service and healing. Each day, Abigail witnessed her mother's example in the Thompson household. Her mother's tireless devotion to Mrs. Eddy and Christian Science healing was plain from the results: patient after patient came into their home sick or troubled, and left healed.[5] "I grew up with my mother's example before me of unswerving loyalty and unbounded admiration for this saintly woman," Miss Thompson wrote. "Mary Baker Eddy was the great inspiration of my mother's life, and her healing fruitage through the years bore unmistakable evidence of the lasting impression her teaching left upon a naturally strong and forceful character."[6]

Abigail's other mentor was her friend and teacher, Mary Baker Eddy. Mrs. Eddy's teachings and writings were Abigail's North Star, and she would spend a lifetime in their study and assimilation. After Mrs. Eddy left Boston and moved to Concord, New Hampshire, teenaged Abigail was a frequent visitor at Mrs. Eddy's home, Pleasant View.

"It has always been my custom to go east for the Annual Meeting [of The Mother Church], and for many years I also made a second trip in the autumn as well. After reaching Boston I would write to Mrs. Eddy and practically always was favored with a call to come to Pleasant View."[7]

Not only had Abigail benefitted from personal visits, she had also been healed by Mrs. Eddy on two occasions.[8] These instantaneous healings — of a hereditary lung condition and a severe hip problem — had a profound impact on both Abigail and her mother, setting a standard for what could be accomplished through Christian Science.

But her friendship with Mrs. Eddy was not all one-sided. Abigail, in turn, brought to Mrs. Eddy the spontaneity and joy of a spirited young woman who at times may have touched Mrs. Eddy's memory of her own youth. There was the occasion, for instance, late in 1887 when Abigail's mother was back in Boston for another class with Mary Baker Eddy. Abigail joined her on this trip. Mrs. Eddy had purchased her home on Commonwealth Avenue and in planning its decoration had enlisted Abigail's assistance in gathering ideas for curtains. Together she and her young friend set off in a carriage through a fashionable part of Boston. Abigail was to scan the windows on one side of the street, Mrs. Eddy took the other. Each was to report to the other any interesting discoveries.

Decades later Abigail wrote of the day's sweet joy and of Mrs. Eddy's appreciation for a child's sense of fun that came from "vying with another person to see which can find the greatest number of objects to call forth exclamations of surprise and approval."[9]

Theirs was the friendship of a teacher and her student, and occasionally of a grandmother spending time with her beloved granddaughter.

"The pictures vanished"

STUDENTS WHO INTERACTED WITH MRS. EDDY OFTEN FOUND THEMSELVES ON the fast track to learning important life lessons. Abigail's life included many such experiences that helped shape the rose branches into what would become her later success.

One such lesson came after a train ride Abigail took to Pleasant View to see Mrs. Eddy. Sitting in her seat absorbed in a book — "an intensely interesting modern story," Abigail called it — she read right up to the instant her train pulled into Concord station.

She closed the book and sped off to her appointment with Mrs. Eddy, the vivid scenes from her book still "surging through [her] consciousness" right up to the moment she was shown into the room where Mrs. Eddy was sitting.

Once Mrs. Eddy spoke to her, there was an immediate change.

"The instant she opened her lips the pictures vanished," Abigail would later write, "and I became so absorbed in the beauty of the spiritual thoughts unfolded by this marvelous woman that I could not open the book on my return trip to Boston, indeed, any interest in the story so completely went out of my mind that the book was never finished."[10]

This incident may have underscored for Abigail how thoroughly the atmosphere of Truth dissolves the atmosphere of fiction — whether that fiction was the vivid images of a compelling story or the vivid images of matter and disease. Indeed, Mary Baker Eddy had defined matter itself as a fiction:

> *Matter, which takes divine power into its own hands and claims to be a creator, is a fiction, in which paganism and lust are so sanctioned by society that mankind has caught their moral contagion.*[11]

Another early lesson came in 1896 while Abigail was on a summer trip to Europe. She wrote Mrs. Eddy from London, requesting that a good photograph of her teacher be mailed to her so she could have a portrait painted in Dresden — a gift for her mother.

Three photos arrived by return mail, along with a letter from Mrs. Eddy addressed to "My dear Miss Thompson" and offering some spiritual perspective on the trip:

> *If you enjoy sight seeing you will no doubt have a pleasant*

time. But bear in mind dear one, that the pleasures of
material sense are treacherous and the spiritual sense of joy
is safe — and Heaven abides in it. May it abide in you.[12]

This was strong meat for a young woman just making her way into the world. But then, perhaps that was the point. Where to focus one's time and attention were critical elements of success — elements that had to be correctly assessed in order to progress in the straight and narrow way. For many people, the learning curve of these life lessons could be half a century. But for Abigail under Mrs. Eddy's tutelage, the bending of the rose branches was clearly under way.

By her late teens Abigail was already preparing for the healing practice. Her ongoing deep study of the Bible and *Science and Health* illumined her way into this healing work, and, like a scientist in her laboratory, she learned each lesson case by case.

Abigail Dyer Thompson, circa 1900.
Photograph, Longyear Museum Collection.

One early instance showed her how important it was to spiritually prepare before even speaking with a patient. Abigail was called upon to meet a complete stranger, a woman passing through Minneapolis, who could see her only between trains. The patient had lost all of her children and was returning from burying her husband. The loss of her family had brought her to the point where she felt she could not go on.

Before meeting this patient Abigail prayed that God's love and power would speak through her to this woman. "The moment I entered her presence," Abigail wrote, "my consciousness seemed illumined with statements of Truth that I had never read or heard before; a veritable floodtide of uplifting thoughts followed in such rapid succession that I had difficulty in giving them utterance."

The woman, whose name is unknown, disappears from the historical record at this point, but this experience showed Abigail the necessity of preparing to meet a patient. During one of her visits to Pleasant View, Abigail related this story to Mrs. Eddy, who commented, "That was true spiritual inspiration, dear."[13]

These were some of the early lessons in their twenty-four-year friendship, from their first meeting in 1886 to Mrs. Eddy's passing in 1910 — a friendship that deeply shaped Abigail's aspirations, helping her to see what one could spiritually achieve.

While still a teenager, Abigail began assisting her mother with her busy healing practice, while at the same time making some "grand demonstrations" of her own, as her mother reported to Mrs. Eddy.[14] When Abigail was nearly twenty, her name joined her mother's in *The Christian Science Journal* as a practitioner in January 1897. Mother and daughter took patients at the Thompson household and studied Mrs. Eddy's writings.

When Mrs. Eddy issued a revision of *Science and Health,* or issued a new publication, the Thompson household quickly purchased it, and a letter of gratitude often followed. After the publication of *Miscellaneous Writings 1883–1896* in 1897, Abigail wrote Mrs. Eddy:

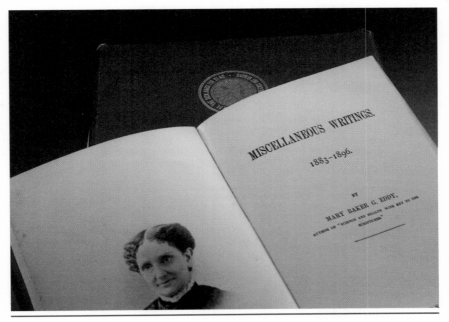

Miscellaneous Writings 1883–1896 by Mary Baker Eddy, first edition, 1897,
Longyear Museum Collection.

> *The little book has come like a heavenly benediction, and each*
> *day as I read from its pages I offer up a prayer of thankfulness*
> *to God, for the blessings it is bringing to every earnest seeker*
> *for Truth, and for the faithful Mother-love which gave it birth.*[15]

In 1902 after Mrs. Eddy issued a major revision of *Science and Health,*
Abigail and her mother sent another note of gratitude:

> *After reading the opening chapters from our inspired text-*
> *book, Science and Health with Key to the Scriptures, with*
> *your recent revisions we hasten to express a few words of lov-*
> *ing gratitude for this new proof of your tireless devotion and*
> *unselfish labor for mankind. Each page is illumined by a*

clearer vision and more exalted demonstration of the power of Divine Love.[16]

Abigail Thompson habitually held Mrs. Eddy's writings to be the standard of truth. When someone expressed an opinion that disagreed with that standard, she refused to accept it. As she told Mrs. Eddy, if she could not find it in her writings, she rejected it, even if the statement in question had come from a prominent Christian Scientist. Mrs. Eddy commended her for this, saying, "Your own interpretation is entirely correct, and in this connection I want to impress upon you one fact, no matter how exalted the position a Christian Scientist may occupy in the movement, never accept what he may say as valid unless you can verify the statement in *Science and Health*."[17]

The class of 1898 — "Love is the healing power"

ALTHOUGH MISS THOMPSON HAD HAD MANY CONVERSATIONS WITH THE Discoverer and Founder of Christian Science since childhood, it was not until 1898 that she sat in a formal class taught by Mrs. Eddy.

The first day, Mrs. Eddy spoke of God as Father, Mother, and Shepherd, which may have been especially meaningful to Miss Thompson, whose father had passed on when she was a child. Mrs. Eddy told the class:

> *Think of God as the Father sustaining and providing for His child; as the Mother upon whose breast the child nestles its little head. The child is fed by the milk of the Word, or think of God as the tender Shepherd tending His flock; seeking out the lost lamb through mire and swamp; calling and listening for the stray lamb's voice; when it is found, carrying it home in His arms; there letting it try its little legs over and over until the lamb is strong enough to be taken out again with the flock....*
>
> *The human man grows away from the human parents; whereas Christian Science teaches us that with the passing*

Mary Baker Eddy. Photograph, S. A. Bowers, Concord, New Hampshire, 1891, Longyear Museum Collection.

years, the spiritual child depends more and more upon his Father-Mother God.[18]

Mrs. Eddy also told them that love was the essential element in healing. Asked to define *love*, Mrs. Eddy said, "I do not mean to love any person or any thing, but just to love." Miss Thompson wrote that the word "love" "filled the room with a meaning that illumined my consciousness in a way I shall never forget." She recorded that Mrs. Eddy said:

Love is the healing power. Love that is impartial. Don't try to love an object, love everything, and see only the reflection of divine Love; that is, see the reflection of God which is loveable.[19]

Mrs. Eddy candidly told the class about how she herself had to learn, sometimes through powerful rebukes to her own human sensibilities. One incident in particular drove home the fact that God was the only healer, a lesson which made a deep and lasting impression on Miss Thompson. In the very early days of Mrs. Eddy's healing work, case after case was instantaneously healed, and one day "with the simplicity of a child she asked God to give her the joy of feeling that she had healed just one case." Almost immediately a call for help arrived — an infant in desperate need of healing. Mrs. Eddy went to the bedside:

> *The realization of Truth came clearly and with great exaltation and she returned home joyous in the thought of having made one demonstration herself; but almost immediately upon entering her door the sister of the little one came running breathlessly to her exclaiming, — "Mother says the baby is dying!" Our Leader immediately closed herself into her bedroom and humbly knelt as she prayed to God for forgiveness for asking that she might become the healing power for even one demonstration; and she said, — "In my anguish I bowed my head until it touched the floor, and when the assurance came again of the loving presence and healing power of God, the child responded instantaneously."* [20]

Thirty years later Miss Thompson could speak of how she had carried in memory this lesson, "because of the deep impression it made on me at the time I heard it." [21]

"I have been busy in your vineyard"

ABOUT HALF A YEAR AFTER THE 1898 NORMAL CLASS, MISS THOMPSON'S healing practice was making rapid strides. She reported to her teacher the following May:

Abigail Dyer Thompson, circa 1900. Photograph, Longyear Museum Collection.

Many months have passed since I last wrote to you, but all the time I have been busy in your vineyard, faithfully watering and pruning each day as love directed; and Mother, more and more do I realize the import of your wonderful teaching last autumn, and my heart overflows with gratitude for the privilege of having been called to sit at your feet.[22]

As with her mother, many of Miss Thompson's cases came from the ranks of those who had been given up by doctors. These cases arrived in her office sometimes within days of receiving a medical diagnosis that offered the people a lifetime of debilitation from some incurable disease. But under Miss Thompson's care, many of these cases resulted in remarkable examples of physical healing, the news of which found its way around town and was generating continued interest in this new religion — interest which her mother had pioneered in the city.

After a doctor had diagnosed William P. Finlay as having a "very bad" case of valvular heart leakage, the eleven-year-old was brought to see Miss Thompson in 1904. Her work overruled this diagnosis with the truth and the result was William found himself completely healed.

"You gave me treatment for two weeks, finally telling me that I was healed," William Finlay wrote to Miss Thompson some two decades later. The healing was confirmed by the same heart specialist when his mother took him back for a follow-up exam. He was pronounced completely healed. "Since that time, of course, Christian Science has been our only help," he wrote.[23]

Under constant medical care from the time he had a severe fall, a Mr. Muir came to see Miss Thompson in 1922. Despite the best medical care, his leg had begun to shrink, and doctors could promise him little more than a life of invalidism. Once Miss Thompson took the case, he quickly improved, and at the end of two weeks had no evidence of lameness. He traveled to the South to spend Christmas with his mother. Six months after this healing, Miss Thompson saw Mr. Muir and was able to bear witness to the completeness of this healing.

"He had gained so much in weight I could scarcely believe it was the same discouraged sick man who, a few months previously, had struggled into my office with a feeling of utter hopelessness and despair," Miss Thompson wrote. "Now, with a merry laugh, he told me he ran up flights of stairs, two steps at a time, with the freedom of a boy, and could dance or take any exercise he pleased with perfect ease."[24]

After a heart specialist determined that Charles Edward Russell, a resident of Washington, D.C., had a severe case of heart disease, he decided to try Christian Science and came to see Miss Thompson. Completely healed, he testified in a letter to her, "I am deeply grateful to you for your patient, persistent and faithful work upon a not very promising subject." An examination by a heart specialist many years later confirmed he had indeed been healed and was in "perfect condition."[25]

All of these cases came to Abigail Dyer Thompson's office with a medical verdict of incurability and ended with a metaphysical triumph.

Notes from a busy practice...

THESE ADDITIONAL TESTIMONIES INDICATE THE RANGE OF CASES Abigail Dyer Thompson dealt with in her practice.

M. B. Hubbard, who was suffering from chronic appendicitis, decided to investigate Christian Science. He had not been able to eat anything except mild breakfast foods. The irony was, he was in Minneapolis to attend a grocers' convention, but, having been urged to call upon Miss Thompson, he found himself sitting in her office, pouring out his heart that he had not eaten solid food for three years.

After she gave him a treatment, she told him to go out and eat any wholesome food he wished. Soon after leaving her office, he felt hungry, so he made a beeline for Minneapolis's Roger's Hotel Café and

Abigail Dyer Thompson, circa 1920.
Photograph, Longyear Museum Collection.

promptly ordered a four-course meal. When he finished, not a morsel was left. He asked Miss Thompson for one more treatment, but later told her that he felt he had been healed from the time of his first visit.[26]

―――――――――

When a girl of seventeen, Ruth Kottke was warned by her dentist, Dr. Arthur Swanson, that she would have false teeth before the age of twenty-five. On another visit three years later, he told her that because of decay he would have to pull many of her teeth. Before the date of this surgery, Ruth went to see Miss Thompson for help. When she returned to the dentist, he compared her teeth against the earlier X-rays and was baffled to find that some of the cavities and decay had disappeared. "This puzzled him very much, he called his assistant, Dr. Cole, in to look," Ruth wrote Miss Thompson. "Dr. Cole couldn't find them…. They couldn't understand what could have happened because they were so sure three years ago that they would have to pull my teeth."[27]

―――――――――

In 1947 Mrs. Olyn Chapin of Minneapolis had just delivered twin boys when the lungs of one of the twins were discovered to be partially filled with liquid. Abigail Dyer Thompson took the case and began to pray. The result was quick and sure, as Mrs. Chapin recalled in a 2004 telephone interview. The pediatric nurse at the facility confirmed the healing when she stuck her head into Mrs. Chapin's room and announced: "Mrs. Chapin, I just wanted you to know that your baby is perfectly fine."[28]

Nine months later, Mrs. Chapin's other twin stopped eating, was listless, and seemed to lose color. Miss Thompson was again called for help. She told Mrs. Chapin that "we are going to take care of him," and that they would depend on God.[29] He was completely healed.

Alfred E. Baker, M.D., C.S.B. Photograph, Marshall, West Chester, Pennsylvania, circa 1884, Longyear Museum Collection.

Although she never married, Miss Thompson's love of children led her to include obstetrics cases in her practice. Her interest in these cases began when her mother attended her second class with Mrs. Eddy, an obstetrics class, in December 1887. Abigail was with her mother in Boston during the class. In 1900 Miss Thompson herself took a course in obstetrics under the auspices of the Christian Science Board of Education taught by Alfred E. Baker, M.D., C.S.B., a former medical doctor who had become a Christian Science practitioner.[30]

Miss Thompson's practice early attracted the attention of Dr. Robert R. Rome, professor of obstetrics at the College of Homeopathic Medicine and Surgery, University of Minnesota.[31] This well-known doctor wanted to learn more about the application of Christian Science to childbirth and asked for an interview with Miss Thompson. In particular, he wanted to know how Christian Science could alleviate fear.

"I endeavored to explain to him the fact that an understanding of the law of God enabled Christian Scientists to overcome many human laws which at times brought great fear and limitation to individuals passing through the experience of childbirth," Miss Thompson later wrote. After the interview, Miss Thompson and Dr. Rome worked together on childbirth cases for several years.[32]

Abigail Dyer Thompson at ground breaking for Second Church of Christ, Scientist,
Minneapolis, July 30, 1951. Photograph, courtesy of
Second Church of Christ, Scientist, Minneapolis.

Among Miss Thompson's papers is an account of Mrs. Claude M. Claghorn
of Minneapolis, whose first child had been stillborn owing to a deformity of
the mother's pelvis. Now, seventeen years later and expecting her second child,
Mrs. Claghorn called upon Miss Thompson for Christian Science treatment. For
months before the birth, Miss Thompson wrote, "earnest work was done to wipe
out the material law":

> *The human belief in the possibility of any deformity was*
> *thoroughly handled, with the result that when the child was*
> *born every condition was absolutely normal.... The last*
> *stage of labor, which before had resulted so disastrously*
> *to the child, was one of the freest and easiest births I have*
> *ever witnessed.*[33]

Into the new century

MISS THOMPSON HAD A SPECIAL PLACE IN HER HEART FOR SECOND CHURCH, Minneapolis, the church Mrs. Eddy had asked her mother to start (see chapter on Emma A. Thompson). Throughout her life Miss Thompson worked hard for its success. She would fill a variety of positions there, including Sunday School teacher, church director, and chairman of the board. Her résumé of church tasks at that branch includes multiple assignments and serving on various committees.

Mrs. Eddy counseled Emma and Abigail Thompson to admit to church membership only such people who would be supportive. Alluding to the murmurers in Exodus 16:2,[34] Mrs. Eddy told them to beware of the ones such as troubled the Israelites on their march to the Promised Land. Several known "murmurers" who applied for membership played successfully on Abigail and Emma's sympathies and were admitted — and just as Mrs. Eddy had warned, they caused trouble.

But Emma and Abigail Thompson learned from the experience, and years later when Miss Thompson was told by a fellow church member some behind-the-back criticism of another, she replied coolly that some people just seemed to be "pudding spoons" — they were always trying to stir things up.[35]

With the passing of her friend and teacher, Mary Baker Eddy, in December of 1910, and then, three years later, the passing of her mother in December of 1913, Abigail Dyer Thompson moved into a different chapter of her lifework. Not being able to turn to these two crucial figures — women who had meant so much to her — she must now, as never before, look to God for guidance in her spiritual work.

This was, after all, the very reason Mrs. Eddy had brought her into the class of 1898 — so that she, along with other members of this second generation of Christian Scientists, could, when the time came, take up various positions in the vineyard, and with authority.

But her mother would be especially missed. The two had lived together as

Abigail Dyer Thompson, circa 1945.
Photograph, courtesy of Second Church of Christ, Scientist, Minneapolis.

a family at 314 Sixth Street, South, Minneapolis, carried on their practices from
the same residence, and attended the same church.

She and her sister, Ella, remained close. But after 1913, Abigail must fill the
void created by the loss of their mother, whose highly successful practice
of Christian Science was seen as responsible for the remarkable growth of
Christian Science in Minneapolis.

Now Miss Thompson would pick up the banner and carry it until the time
of her passing in 1957. This she did with remarkable facility. After her mother
passed on, Miss Thompson moved into Minneapolis's Leamington Hotel. Her
large apartment served as living quarters, office, and even classroom.

One student, Dorothy Ann Hodgman, who attended her 1948 Primary class,
recalled Miss Thompson standing in her living room at a little lectern that held
her teaching notes in front of the thirty students. She recalled her strong voice
filling the room.[36] "The thing that was so interesting," Mrs. Hodgman said,
"[was how] large her apartment was — she *always* had a full class of thirty,
and she had thirty chairs in her living room in the Leamington Hotel and she

had a grand piano, or a baby grand probably, also."[37]

Mrs. Hodgman was first introduced to Miss Thompson when, as a little girl, she was enrolled at the Sunday School of Second Church of Christ, Scientist, Minneapolis, where Miss Thompson was her Sunday School teacher. One evening she came down with a case of strep throat and could not swallow. Her mother called Miss Thompson for help. The next morning, she had "no trace" of a sore throat.[38] Mrs. Hodgman remembered this healing, and when she was a grown woman and seeking out a teacher, she naturally turned to the person who had helped her when a little girl.

By the third and fourth decades of the twentieth century, the name Abigail Dyer Thompson had risen in esteem in the Minneapolis field, and beyond, to nearly that of her mother. Her healing work at this time showed that she had gained the dominion "through love" that Mrs. Eddy had spoken about in the class of 1898.

When medical X-rays showed a broken hip with four distinct fractures, Mrs. Agnes C. DeGroodt decided to seek out Christian Science for help. She came to see Miss Thompson and the result was, she was completely healed. In her testimony the Minnesota woman said:

> My thought was lifted above the claim of age, thus breaking
> the laws of limitation and fear usually held over one who
> has passed her eighty-sixth birthday. Words cannot express
> my gratitude for this beautiful healing.[39]

In a statement corroborating this healing, her daughter, Mabel DeGroodt, reported that when her mother's bandages were removed, the doctor said she was in better condition "than the average young woman." Mabel wrote:

> Today (one year from the date of the fall) she is going up and
> down stairs [and] getting in and out of the bathtub
> alone ... attending church services, and lectures with a sense of
> freedom and joy that makes us bow our heads and hearts in
> humble gratitude to God.[40]

Abigail Dyer Thompson, C.S.B.
Photograph, Gene Garrett,
Minneapolis, circa 1930,
Longyear Museum Collection.

Emma C. Shipman, C.S.B., circa 1950.
Photograph, Longyear Museum
Collection.

After Margaret Benson's father became ill while on a fishing trip, he was taken to a hospital and put into surgery for what doctors diagnosed as a ruptured appendix. When these doctors determined the case was beyond their capacity to cure, the family urgently turned to Christian Science and Abigail Dyer Thompson for help. Miss Thompson turned to God and went to work refuting this medical diagnosis and evaluation. "How well I remember her calm and positive assurance that my father would recover!" Mrs. Benson wrote in her testimony of this healing.

Two days later, when Mrs. Benson went to visit her father, she found him sitting up in bed, taking pictures with his camera. "What a joyous morning for our family!" Mrs. Benson said. "In addition to the physical healing, he found that he no longer had a desire to smoke.... Reaching out for help, my parents had confidence in Miss Thompson's work, and through absent treatments alone, the healing came."[41]

We knew Mary Baker Eddy

IN 1942 ABIGAIL DYER THOMPSON AND HER GOOD FRIEND AND FELLOW 1898 class member Emma Shipman, C.S.B., were asked by the Christian Science Board of Directors to address the June 1942 General Activities meeting after Annual Meeting. Both were now Christian Science teachers and were asked to offer some of their firsthand experiences from having known Mrs. Eddy.

As the two prepared their talks, their letters flew back and forth.

"I am sure you know how grateful and happy it makes me to have you on the same program with me for no one of all our dear Leader's students means quite so much to me as you do," Miss Thompson wrote her friend.[42]

Their letters spoke of how each would focus the subject matter of their respective talks so as not to cover the same ground.

Other important matters were discussed in the female vernacular:

"Have you decided what you are going to wear on the platform?" Miss Thompson asked her friend. "I have thought of using a long light blue silk with lace top to match which I wore in my last association. Does this seem appropriate to you?"[43]

Five days later Miss Shipman's reply came from Pittsfield, Massachusetts, on Hotel Wendell stationery. "Your blue silk will be lovely and just the right thing I am sure," she wrote. "The sample enclosed is of my dress. It is long and I wore it a year ago at my Association meeting."[44]

The Board had requested all talks for the meeting to be held to twenty minutes, meaning the women were each held to a mere two thousand words. Each was concerned the other would not have enough time to tell her full story, and so each, independent of the other, wrote to the Board of Directors offering to give up her time to the other. As it turned out, each did speak that evening as planned.

One of Miss Thompson's letters to Miss Shipman includes an outline of the topics she had to choose from. She told her friend she was having trouble deciding what would be of most interest from her list of experiences with Mrs. Eddy. These included her first meeting, childhood experiences, her two healings, and tributes Mrs. Eddy paid her mother. The talks given that day by Abigail Dyer Thompson and Emma C. Shipman were published in the *Christian Science Sentinel* and later republished in *We Knew Mary Baker Eddy.*[45]

If Miss Thompson's understanding of Mrs. Eddy began with such pleasant childhood experiences as the "curtain expedition," it would come to fruition in a deeper and more profound understanding of her as Leader. An interesting piece of evidence is found during the so-called "Next Friends" suit in 1907.[46] If successful, the suit could have ended Mrs. Eddy's leadership of the Christian Science movement.

Before the suit was settled, Miss Thompson had a dream that may indicate what she was perceiving metaphysically during this crisis. In the dream she stood on a mountain overlooking a beautiful valley, which had grown "dark and foreboding" with storm clouds. Against the darkness, "a cross of light" moved slowly, serenely, to the west, the storm clouds retreating before it. The dream then depicted Mrs. Eddy, "head uplifted and hands clasped as though in prayer," moving "calmly and majestically," following the cross and disappearing in the west. The dream ended with "a great rainbow...bathing the entire valley in a glow of indescribable loveliness."[47]

When she awoke, Miss Thompson spent considerable time pondering the dream. Visiting Mrs. Eddy at Pleasant View, she recounted the dream. Mrs. Eddy replied, "That is an allegory of what I have been passing through."[48]

The incident speaks powerfully of the friendship and trust between the two women. The dream itself and Mrs. Eddy's affirmation of it as an allegory that rang true suggest that Miss Thompson was seeing deeper into Mrs. Eddy's experience. That Mary Baker Eddy carved out time to visit with her during this critical period illustrates her appreciation of this young student. And that Miss Thompson felt free to confide the dream underscores the trust between the two.

"To see a goal and move steadily towards it without wavering"

IF THE SEED OF MISS THOMPSON'S DESIRE TO BECOME A CHRISTIAN SCIENCE practitioner was planted when she was a little girl, under the instruction of her friend and teacher, Mary Baker Eddy, and her mother, Emma Thompson, it was brought to fruition through decades of selfless devotion — an obedience to and demonstration of the truth she was learning from her study of *Science and Health* and the Bible.

At the time of her passing in 1957, Abigail Dyer Thompson had spent about sixty years focused on attaining this high goal. Like many of the other pioneers, her life included moments of self-doubt overcome, many self-sacrifices made on behalf of others, many limitations surmounted. But also like many of the other pioneer Christian Scientists, she would discover that, in turning to God, these trials provided the very mechanism that would elevate her and lead her to gain the dominion she sought. From that place of dominion she could then help lift others — hundreds, perhaps thousands, out of the bondage of sickness, pain, fear, and sin.

If there was a key to her success, it might very well be captured in that single sentence she spoke in a 1933 report she gave to her beloved Second Church of Christ, Scientist, Minneapolis, that is quoted near the beginning of this chapter:

> The genius of progress is really the genius of work, — the ability to see a goal and move steadily towards it without wavering, in the spirit of Paul when he said, "this one thing I do" (Phil 3:13).[49]

Abigail Dyer Thompson's singular life of love for Christian Science and Mary Baker Eddy as Leader resulted in a life of devotion, a life that bore much fruit through holding to a single focus — *"this one thing I do."*

JANETTE E. WELLER

FINDING HEAVEN, FINDING HOME

Janette E. Weller, C.S.D. Photograph, S. A. Bowers, Concord,
New Hampshire, circa 1885, Longyear Museum Collection.

JANETTE E. WELLER
FINDING HEAVEN, FINDING HOME

ON A SPRING DAY IN 1884, JANETTE EASTMAN WELLER WALKED UP TO THE
front door of 571 Columbus Avenue, Boston, rang the doorbell, then stood back
and waited.[1]

A few weeks earlier, this New Hampshire schoolteacher, then in her mid-
forties, awoke one morning to find herself completely healed of tuberculosis
after twenty years of suffering. She knew exactly what had brought about this
healing. She had spent the previous three weeks studying a new book she had
just bought, *Science and Health with Key to the Scriptures* by Mary Baker Eddy.

"Free as a bird," as she now referred to herself, Mrs. Weller decided to
go find the book's author, a trip that took her from her home in Littleton,
New Hampshire, 160 miles south to Boston and to the front door of the Massachusetts Metaphysical College, where Mrs. Eddy taught Christian Science.

When the door opened, Mrs. Weller was allowed inside, but only to speak
to one of Mrs. Eddy's students. Mrs. Eddy herself was not to be disturbed. While
talking to this student, Mrs. Weller asked many questions about this reinstate-
ment of Christian healing. The student answered them, then ushered her
back toward the front door, where she was given an opportunity to see a
portrait of Mrs. Eddy in the reception room of the College.

As they entered the room, there on a chair sat Mary Baker Eddy herself.

"Walk right in," Mrs. Eddy said, reaching out her hand in welcome. "What
a power of Mind it was that brought me downstairs. I was at my desk, writing as
busily as ever I was in my life, when, suddenly, I laid aside my pen, came down

Mary Baker Eddy. Photograph, H. G. Smith Studio, Boston, 1886, Longyear Museum Collection.

here and waited — I did not know what for."[2] Then ensued a conversation, at the end of which came an invitation for Mrs. Weller to join Mrs. Eddy's next class.

The life of this New England schoolteacher turned tailor's seamstress was turned yet again that day onto a new path, a path that would lead her to take three courses of instruction on Christian Science with its Discoverer and Founder: Primary class, beginning on September 2, 1884; Obstetrics class, beginning December 5, 1887; and Normal class, on May 21, 1889. In these classes, she would be shown the scientific system of Christian healing — the system that had healed her, and was transforming her life.

Later, as a prominent practitioner of Christian Science, Mrs. Weller would become one of the early proponents of this system, helping to lay foundation stones of Christian Science in northern New Hampshire, Philadelphia, and Binghamton, New York. She preached at Christian Science services in Littleton, New Hampshire, and taught the first class in Christian Science in Spokane, Washington. From the time of her move to Boston in March of 1893, however, Mrs. Weller focused on her work as a practitioner, although Mrs. Eddy would call upon her for special tasks, from caring for a relative, to gathering copies of Mrs. Eddy's articles from *The Christian Science Journal* for publication in *Miscellaneous Writings*.[3]

Mary Baker Eddy had many loyal students, and as the Christian Science movement grew, she had many thousands who called her Leader. But there were few that she herself could call friend. Janette Weller was one of them.

As Mrs. Weller returned to her New Hampshire home that day from this first meeting with Mrs. Eddy, she knew one thing for certain: Jesus' promise, "seek, and ye shall find; knock, and it shall be opened unto you,"[4] had just proven itself true. A door had opened and Mrs. Weller had walked through. She knew she was now taking some of her first steps in a new place, a place that she sensed held great promise.

Perhaps this is what St. Paul meant by being made new in Christ.[5]

"Leaving *nothing* and finding *all*"

"TO LEAVE ALL FOR CHRIST," MRS. EDDY WOULD WRITE MRS. WELLER ABOUT four years after their first meeting, "is leaving *nothing* and finding *all*."[6]

Some may stumble over those first three words, fearing what life might look like after "leaving all." But Mrs. Weller's life had seen so much sorrow and disappointment that Mrs. Eddy's admonition sounded more like an invitation — a promise to come find true happiness and a genuine home. It was as if Jesus' words to the Samaritan woman at Jacob's well at Sychar had come alive: "If thou knewest the gift of God ..."[7]

Born on July 4, 1840, to Scottish-Irish father Samuel Umphrey Gibson and Mercy Gates Hoskins, Janette was wrenched from everything she knew and loved when, at three years old, her parents separated and she was sent to live with her father's sister, Mrs. Margaret Eastman, in Lyman, New Hampshire.[8]

"I had no home, no happy childhood," Mrs. Weller wrote Mrs. Eddy. "I longed for a home on earth which is but the type of the home in heaven (harmony) for which you longed, and lived, and have brought to us all if we are faithful to your teachings."[9]

After high school, Janette was able to attend two spring terms at McIndoes Falls Academy in Vermont. At the age of seventeen, she was essentially on her own. She taught eight terms in the Littleton public schools so successfully that at the completion of each term she was asked to stay on. At about the age of twenty, she found employment in a Littleton tailor shop, where in just fifteen months she demonstrated mastery at sewing pants, vests, and coats, the latter generally requiring seven years' apprenticeship. The skills gained in the tailor shop did not become obsolete when she became a Christian Scientist: she put them to good use in assisting Mary Baker Eddy in practical ways with her wardrobe at Pleasant View.

In 1861, at the age of twenty-one, she married Copeland Franklin George Weller, an artist, coach painter, and well-known stereoscopic photographer, specializing in views of the White Mountains. He passed on sixteen years later at the age of forty-four.[10] The couple had a daughter, Fontenella ("Fontie"), born January 4, 1867.

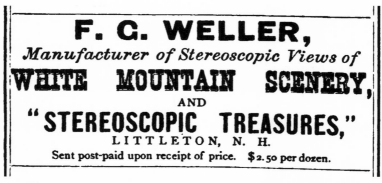

F. G. WELLER,
Manufacturer of Stereoscopic Views of
WHITE MOUNTAIN SCENERY,
AND
"STEREOSCOPIC TREASURES,"
L I T T L E T O N, N. H.
Sent post-paid upon receipt of price. $2.50 per dozen.

Franklin G. Weller advertisement in *The New Hampshire Register, Farmer's Almanac and Business Directory for 1873.*

In 1882 the widowed Janette married F. A. Robinson — "a druggist by profession and a hypochondriac by nature and choice," according to Mrs. Weller.[11] Eight years later, as she was becoming increasingly active in the practice of Christian Science, Robinson filed for divorce. The divorce proceedings, as noted below, became a virtual attack on Christian Science, with public examination of Mrs. Robinson and her Christian Science practice.

Stereoscopic image of Fontenella Weller posed as Columbia. Photograph, Franklin G. Weller, Littleton, New Hampshire, 1873, Library of Congress.

After this unjust, humiliating experience, Mrs. Weller joined her daughter, Fontie, in Spokane, Washington, who also was a student of Christian Science. Fontie had married a Henry Fitch of Somerville, Massachusetts, and the couple moved to Spokane, after Henry accepted a position with the Washington National Bank. While in Spokane, Mrs. Weller launched Christian Science work in that city. In January 1892, Fontie gave birth to a daughter, but sadly, both Fontie and her infant daughter passed on three months later.[12] Again bereft of family, Janette Weller returned east in July 1892, settling first in her hometown of Littleton, but relocating to Boston in the spring of 1893.

The tragic parallels between Mrs. Eddy's and Mrs. Weller's personal lives — early widowhood, unhappy second marriage, loss of child through death or circumstance — perhaps drew them together into a unique friendship. Each could appreciate something of the depths of what the other had experienced of human loss and loneliness; where others might sympathize, they *knew*. The result was that Mrs. Eddy's letters to Mrs. Weller could carry a special tenderness that sits scattered throughout her sentences like oases of love and home.

In one such letter, Mrs. Eddy tells Mrs. Weller, who at that time was still married to F. A. Robinson: "Hope home is sweet to you the faithful one...."[13] In another, Mrs. Weller, now divorced and after the passing of her daughter and

Pleasant View, home of Mary Baker Eddy in Concord, New Hampshire, 1892–1908. Photograph, circa 1905, Longyear Museum Collection.

granddaughter, received an invitation to spend a late summer's day with Mrs. Eddy at Pleasant View. The invitation included the promise: "I want you to see my house and have some corn and peas, cucumbers and raspberries. Is not this a strange want for me? Well come, and I'll tell you of sweeter things."[14]

The following summer, another harvest brought yet another gift. This time Mrs. Eddy sent baskets filled with her garden's bounty to both Mrs. Weller and fellow Christian Science worker Laura Sargent. Such were some of the fruits that began to flourish in Mrs. Weller's life.

Early hardships had developed in Mrs. Weller the raw materials of hard work, dedication, and loyalty. Just as she had shown an aptitude for learning when working as a seamstress at the Littleton tailor shop, she now applied this same determination and discipline to a deep, concentrated study of *Science and Health*. Indeed, when she was back home in New Hampshire after meeting its author for the first time, Mrs. Weller used the next five months to prepare herself diligently for the September 1884 Primary class with Mrs. Eddy.

"I literally hungered and thirsted for the righteousness which is taught so simply, and made so practical, on every page of that inspired book," Mrs. Weller wrote of this period. "The more I read, the more I wanted to read."[15]

As she began to understand something of Mrs. Eddy's discovery as explained in *Science and Health,* Mrs. Weller's friends commented that during this period they were being healed merely by talking to her. Indeed, one man reported that contact with Mrs. Weller had healed him of a blow to the head from the butt of an axe.

"Several times, during the summer, people almost *accusingly* acknowledged to me that I had made them feel better, curing them of headaches, and so forth, while I conversed with them," Mrs. Weller wrote. "These experiences puzzled me, for I had no idea how to apply what I had been reading to the healing of sickness."[16]

"Is man *anything* but obedience?"

TO SIT IN A CLASS TAUGHT BY MARY BAKER EDDY WAS NOT JUST TO BE A STUDENT learning from an instructor; as Mrs. Weller discovered, it was also to be brought under Mrs. Eddy's spiritual *expectation.* Much was given, much would be required.

"Mother," Mrs. Weller once asked Mrs. Eddy, "is man *anything* but obedience?"

Mrs. Eddy raised both her hands and said, "Not a thing, and what a growth."[17]

Here lay an important aspect of Mrs. Weller's success. If healing was the outgrowth of understanding the spiritual truth of being, then the way to this understanding was a disciplined willingness to learn it and then live it. One lived it by obedience to Mrs. Eddy's teachings. Mrs. Eddy certainly expected as much from her students. Mrs. Weller's writings indicate that she seemed to grasp early on that the discipline of Christian discipleship was essential to progress.

Indeed, Mrs. Eddy saw in Mrs. Weller someone who, although not exempt from making mistakes, nonetheless learned from them and strove to remain obedient and to watch. After a meeting with Mrs. Weller at Pleasant View in the mid-1890s, Mrs. Eddy commended what she saw in her student:

> When you were last here you seemed so near my heart that I did not need to speak to you. This is a phenomenon that always since I discovered Science has followed me in Science. When a student comes to see me and I find them so right, if any one else is with them I can only talk to them that are not so clear.... My life is made up of self sacrifice. I only seem to achieve, the little that I do accomplish, not for myself but for the Students.[18]

"What was I to do...?"

IT WAS ONE THING TO BE LIFTED UP IN MRS. EDDY'S PRIMARY CLASS TO SEE something of spiritual reality — many of her students reported catching a glimpse of the spiritual nature of God's creation and His perfect man. But it was another matter for a Primary student to apply these truths successfully to a patient in need of healing. So, after the eighth day of the September 1884 Primary class, Mrs. Eddy asked each of the nine students to heal someone by the next session.

Student Weller took the news somewhat anxiously: "What was I to do in such a dilemma?" she wondered.[19]

Returning to her boardinghouse, Mrs. Weller found the friend she was staying with complaining about a physical ailment. She took the case and began to pray, but soon realized that in the eight days of lessons thus far, Mrs. Eddy had not yet explained specifically how to heal a case of disease.

But as Mrs. Weller looked back at what Mrs. Eddy had taught the class during those first eight days, she concluded the teaching contained everything she needed to bring about healing. "It had all been about God and His image and likeness, man, and that there was no sickness in *either* of *them*."[20] Mrs. Weller then discovered her patient was completely healed — a healing that increased Mrs. Weller's confidence in the truth of Christian Science and in her ability to demonstrate it. Just as Jesus had sent his disciples — without him — into the surrounding towns to heal the sick, in part, perhaps, to develop in them just such confidence,[21] so Mrs. Eddy, too, nudged her students out into the deeper waters of spiritual demonstration, where a student began to see what he or she was capable of achieving through Christian Science.

Indeed, Mrs. Eddy made it clear that Christian Science could be understood only through healing. "Science is not susceptible of being held as a mere theory," she wrote in *No and Yes.*[22] Mrs. Weller witnessed a most interesting discussion of this very point play itself out during a Thanksgiving dinner.

Mrs. Eddy sometimes invited those without a place to go for Thanksgiving — she endearingly called them "orphans" — to come to her house for dinner. Mrs. Weller spent three such Thanksgivings at Mrs. Eddy's dinner table.

In November 1886 Mrs. Eddy hosted a Thanksgiving dinner, to which she had invited a number of "orphans." These included Janette Weller (then Mrs. Robinson); the Reverend William I. Gill of Lawrence, Massachusetts, a Methodist preacher turned Christian Scientist; his wife and daughter; and Mrs. Eddy's sister-in-law, Mary Ann Cook Baker (widow of her eldest brother Samuel).[23]

It was an interesting group. In Mrs. Eddy's April Primary class half a year earlier,[24] the Reverend Gill had shown himself to be a promising student and Mrs. Eddy quickly sent him into the front ranks of the work. He was made assistant pastor of the Church of Christ (Scientist) in Boston to preach the new religion on Sundays when Mrs. Eddy was too busy herself to preach, and in August he became editor of the *Journal.*

After dinner, when they were sitting in the parlor, the fireworks began. The conversation turned to theology, and the former clergyman, no doubt somewhat protective of his hard-won knowledge of Christian theology, peppered Mrs. Eddy with question after question centered on the assertion that God, to be omniscient, must know evil.

Mrs. Weller observed that his theoretical approach failed to grasp Mrs. Eddy's underlying metaphysical point. After the conversation had gone on for a while, Mrs. Eddy, seated next to the minister on the sofa, turned to him and fired: "Brother Gill, you will *never* understand these things until you heal the sick."[25]

This was an eye-opening moment for Mrs. Weller, who came away from the dinner having gained what she called a "vital point in Christian Science" — a point she realized had to be understood by every Christian Scientist.[26] The Reverend Gill, unable to grasp this point, found himself increasingly at logger-heads with Mrs. Eddy and her teachings.

The Gill comet had streaked across the Christian Science horizon that year but burned out a few months later. In February 1887, a mere three months after the Thanksgiving dinner, the Boston church dismissed Gill as assistant pastor, and several days later, when it was learned that he had been attacking Christian Science and Mrs. Eddy, he was expelled from the Christian Scientist Association. Within a few days he joined forces with the anti-Christian Scientists that included Edward J. Arens.

After considering the defections of Gill and others, Mrs. Weller humbly wondered in a letter written the next summer to Calvin Frye: "What am I that I should expect to stand, where so many have fallen whom I have believed were so far beyond me in understanding?" She vowed, "I am trying to take heed lest I fall. And my constant prayer is that I may be one of the faithful."[27]

Perhaps an early indication that the way was strait and narrow and few there were that found it,[28] was Mrs. Weller's observation that from the time of about three years after the 1884 Primary class she attended, she never again heard the names of the other eight students mentioned as being in the ranks of Christian Scientists. Of that class of nine, Mrs. Weller alone left a positive name in the history of Christian Science.[29]

"Do you find any difficulty in healing?"

MRS. EDDY NURTURED HER STUDENTS, AND ESPECIALLY DURING THEIR EARLY years of practice it was not unusual for them to receive private interviews and letters of encouragement. Half a year into the full-time practice, Mrs. Weller received such instruction from her teacher — this time, a short treatise on healing, contained in one of about forty letters Mrs. Eddy sent her student over the years. "Do you find any difficulty in healing?" the teacher asked. She continued:

> *If so, strike for the higher sense of the* nothingness of matter. *Do not care to search into causation there for there is no cause and no effect in matter;* all is Mind, *perfect and eternal. Whenever you treat a patient include in your understanding of the case that no ignorant or malicious mind can affect the case. There* is no relapse. *Science tells us this — is all it manifests.*[30]

Mrs. Eddy ended her letter with the admonition, written just above her signature: "These are the rules for you to work out every hour of your life." And two years later when her student was in the midst of what Mrs. Weller called the "thickest of the battle," Mrs. Eddy wrote to offer support: "Our Father is keeping guard over these hours. He knows them only to reach them by the eternal law of right and justice. His laws and His love sustain us."[31] Nearly a decade later, in September 1895, Mrs. Eddy advised her: "You cannot take [a] more direct way to success in healing than to break the so-called laws of sin. This you have done and so made the way for others."[32]

Some Christian Science pioneers left behind detailed accounts of their healing work. Mrs. Weller, alas, provided very few details about her practice. There are tantalizing hints as to her activity, found in her letters to Mrs. Eddy and Calvin Frye, in her reminiscence,[33] and in the pages of *The Christian Science Journal*. For instance, a Mrs. S. E. Barnum from Mrs. Weller's hometown of Littleton wrote Mrs. Eddy a testimony of healing, reprinted in the *Journal*, in which Mrs. Weller was the practitioner.

Mrs. Barnum's daughter Mabel had come down with rheumatism after a throat condition worsened to the point where the little girl was pale and lame:

Janette E. Weller, circa 1900.
Photograph, Longyear Museum Collection.

At the end of three weeks we were seriously alarmed. I called a physician, who prescribed for her, and said it was a bad case of rheumatism. I followed his directions, but she grew rapidly worse, her feet and limbs swelling badly, and her suffering becoming very intense. For three weeks we were without sleep. The night previous to calling Mrs. Robinson I was unable to change Mabel's position in the least, for she screamed if I attempted to do so. The moment Mrs. Robinson came into the room Mabel became quiet, and she has never complained of pain since. She immediately sank into a sweet sleep, and after two hours' rest sat up and had her hair combed. She then washed her own face, neck, and hands, and called for her breakfast, of which she partook as heartily as usual. Since then she has not missed a meal. After two days' treatment she went about the house, passing through the hall when the outer door was wide open and the mercury at zero. Through the fall and winter scarcely a day passed that Mabel did not complain of her bad feelings; but this error has disappeared.[34]

"He tried you in the fire"

IN MAY OF 1889, MRS. WELLER ENROLLED, AT MRS. EDDY'S REQUEST, IN THE Normal class, the training for becoming a teacher of Christian Science. But she ran into a financial problem, the resolution of which illustrates Mrs. Weller's strong sense of integrity.

Finding herself unable to pay the tuition, Mrs. Weller gave her teacher a note for the amount, and as she earned money, she sent Mrs. Eddy small payments. One day a receipt from Mrs. Eddy arrived in the mail acknowledging that the debt had been paid. While Mrs. Eddy had not asked for interest, her student was determined to pay it as well. "I said to myself, 'She'll get that interest some time, if it's possible for me to pay it.'"[35]

That time came in the autumn of 1893 after Mrs. Weller sold her New Hampshire home and moved to Boston to serve as a practitioner there. She sat down, calculated the amount, and sent Mrs. Eddy the final payment. She said she felt happy doing this.[36] In her return letter, Mrs. Eddy commended Mrs. Weller for her conscientiousness, telling her that what she had done was "most encouraging" and "rare." Thanking God for Mrs. Weller's prosperity and saying that she was not at all surprised by it, Mrs. Eddy continued:

> He tried you in the fire. He loves to deliver His children from
> the depths. He chooses them not in worldly prosperity but in
> the midst of affliction. Thus has He accepted you, dear one.[37]

Such incidents as Mrs. Weller's determination to pay the interest reveal something of her underlying ethic of responsibility and accountability.

Mrs. Weller also had an acute awareness of her mistakes and a willingness to quickly repent after being corrected by Mrs. Eddy — a quality shared by the students who remained loyal to their Leader. For instance, in 1896, after an unsuccessful attempt to assist Mrs. Eddy, Mrs. Weller wrote Calvin Frye that she felt "much grieved" that her failure — probably to procure clothes that fit Mrs. Eddy — had caused trouble for her teacher, who "has done ten thousand times more for us than we have yet the faintest conception of." She added:

O, I know there is but one way and that is to press on more
earnestly and with a more self-sacrificing spirit than ever
before.... I know I will have every experience I need to bring
my thought into subjection to divine Will.[38]

In an earlier letter to Mrs. Eddy, Mrs. Weller had put it more bluntly: "If I need to be whipped, I *want* to be."[39] Instances like these run through her letters, showing her willingness to learn. Just as she had shown years earlier while working at the tailor shop in Littleton, New Hampshire, Mrs. Weller's eagerness to follow instructions, even in regard to details that others might regard as too exacting, proved a great aid to her success.

"The most agonizing hours of my whole life"

"TRIALS TEACH MORTALS NOT TO LEAN ON A MATERIAL STAFF, — A BROKEN reed, which pierces the heart," Mrs. Eddy writes in the chapter "Marriage" in *Science and Health.*[40]

While in the midst of her pioneering work in Philadelphia in 1890, Mrs. Weller (then Mrs. Robinson) received notification that her home life was to be shattered for a third time: her husband had filed for divorce. She returned to Littleton only to face a court proceeding in which the strategy of her husband's attorney was to discredit her and thus relieve his client from having to pay her any alimony. Thus, the trial that ensued was spun around the defendant's practice of Christian Science. Essentially, he put the religion and her practice of it on trial.

With the courtroom filled with curious townspeople, Mrs. Robinson found herself under fire from opposing counsel in what amounted to a ferocious examination. But this student of Mary Baker Eddy saw in this trial an opportunity to demonstrate Christian Science.

When asked by counsel, hoping to make a fool of her, to tell the court how she gave a Christian Science treatment, she obliged.

She recited these treatments out loud and did this with a sense of joy: "My whole thought and prayer was that I might be able to impress upon others the fact that a new dispensation had come to the world through Christian Science."

She found it indispensable to prepare spiritually for each day's court proceeding. Mrs. Robinson even held her own against the opposing lawyer, who was doing his best to fluster and confuse her. Asked what she would do as a Christian Science practitioner about a case of worms, she told the courtroom she would pray for the case. When the lawyer asked her what she would do with the worms, she replied: "*I* would take care of the patient and let *you* take care of the worms," sending the courtroom into a burst of laughter.

But in her account of that day, Mrs. Weller confessed that while court participants and observers were enjoying the spectacle, she was not. These were the most "agonizing hours" she had ever passed through. She said that on an especially difficult day of the trial she paced back and forth in her house while saying aloud: "I thank God that I am worthy of such persecution."[41]

A few weeks after the divorce was finalized, Mrs. Weller visited Mrs. Eddy at Pleasant View, where Mrs. Eddy extended her sympathy for what her student had just gone through. She startled Mrs. Weller, though, by stating that she pitied Mr. Robinson more greatly than she did her, because while Mrs. Weller had Christian Science to comfort her, he had nothing. Mrs. Weller told her teacher that while she did not feel bitterness toward her persecutors for the "heart-rending and unjust" experiences that she had endured, she acknowledged that she had been "constantly tormented with a burning desire to be justified before the world."

Mrs. Weller said that for many months she felt an "intense longing for self-justification" until one Sunday, while attending a Christian Science church service, she realized that her justification would inevitably result in the condemnation of another. With this insight came a realization that self-justification was "the highest sense of revenge." Mrs. Weller later told this to Mrs. Eddy, who confirmed her assessment.[42]

This trial may well have reminded Mrs. Weller of a private conversation she had had with Mrs. Eddy six years earlier about another marriage that ended in divorce. While attending the Primary class, Mrs. Weller mentioned that after reading *Science and Health* she had healed a Mr. Patterson in Littleton of a blow to the head from the butt of an axe. Since she had known so little of Christian Science at the time, could this really have been a Christian Science healing, she asked her teacher. Mrs. Eddy responded in front of the class, "Certainly; always give credit to Truth."[43]

Mrs. Eddy then asked Mrs. Weller whether the man had been a dentist, and she answered no but that there had been a dentist in the town named Daniel Patterson. When the class ended, Mrs. Eddy invited Mrs. Weller to come to dinner. Sitting in the parlor, Mrs. Eddy asked her about Dr. Patterson. She told Mrs. Eddy that his conduct had caused townspeople to question his morality.

Then Mrs. Eddy dropped a bombshell: "He was my husband."

Mrs. Weller was stunned and did not want to hear more. The association of such a person as Daniel Patterson with Mary Baker Eddy was unimaginably disconcerting to Mrs. Weller. Mrs. Eddy, however, explained: "If it had not been for that man, I should never have given the world Christian Science."[44]

Six years after that conversation, Mrs. Weller, now faced with her divorce,

Dr. Daniel Patterson, second husband of Mary Baker Eddy.
Detail from photograph, circa 1850, Longyear Museum Collection.

would also experience some of the depths of human heartlessness and at the same time grow under it, learning how to work her way through the legal proceedings, which had turned into an attack on Christian Science.

"All that I know of God, good, has come to me through *your* self-sacrifice"

WHEN MRS. EDDY FELT THE NEED FOR SOME DAYS' RESPITE AWAY FROM BOSTON in August 1888, she invited Mrs. Weller to join her at the White Mountain House, New Hampshire.

As Mrs. Eddy's secretary, Calvin Frye, and soon-to-be-adopted son, Ebenezer Foster, were registering at the primitive hotel desk, Mrs. Weller noted that Mrs. Eddy was surveying the rustic scene of the one-hundred-year-old country inn, complete with wavering, uneven floorboards and warped doors. "Oh, how beautiful," Mrs. Eddy exclaimed.[45]

Mrs. Eddy and Mrs. Weller stayed in an adjoining two-room century-old cottage, with plain wooden chairs, green shades and white muslin curtains, floors covered with straw matting and woolen area rugs, and a wood-burning heating stove in the larger room. Mrs. Weller noted that Mrs. Eddy preferred the smaller, nine-by-eleven-foot room, and so Mrs. Weller occupied the larger, twenty-by-twenty-foot space. During these days of rest away from Boston, Mrs. Eddy confided in Mrs. Weller, talking to her "of many things that were causing her great anxiety."[46]

While there, Mrs. Eddy gave an address at the nearby luxury hotel, Fabyan House. Ten years later, in her dedicatory message to a church in the White Mountains, Mrs. Eddy recalled this visit:

> In 1888 I visited these mountains and spoke to an attentive audience collected in the hall at the Fabyan House. Then and there I foresaw this hour, and spoke of the little church to be in the midst of the mountains, closing my remarks with the words of Mrs. Hemans: —

Fabyan House, White Mountains, New Hampshire.
Engraving from *Snow's Hand Book of Northern Pleasure Travel,* 1879.

> *For the strength of the hills, we bless Thee,*
> *Our God, our fathers' God!*[47]

While Mrs. Weller was blessed by her close association with this extraordinary teacher and friend, Mrs. Eddy in turn benefitted from the many tasks Mrs. Weller was able to perform for her. Mrs. Weller demonstrated an ability to provide Mrs. Eddy, who often had no time to try on garments for fitting, with clothes that not only pleased Mrs. Eddy but also fit her, thus allowing the Leader of Christian Science to focus attention on her labor for her church. After one such successful endeavor, Mrs. Eddy wrote her:

> *My dress is made and trimmed as beautiful as a painting. It*
> *has the effect of embroidery. The fit is perfect.*[48]

Mrs. Weller took note of Mrs. Eddy's comfort. Being shown around Pleasant View by Mrs. Eddy's maid, Mrs. Weller noticed a "shabby-looking" patchwork quilt at the foot of Mrs. Eddy's bed. "I felt like crying," Mrs. Weller later wrote.[49] On her return to Boston, she promptly bought an eiderdown quilt and had it sent by express to Mrs. Eddy, who noted that the gift was particularly

Janette E. Weller. Oil on canvas portrait from life by Carol Aus, 1919,
Longyear Museum Collection.

timely: "Oh if you knew how it was appreciated by me at this special time you could see Why."[50]

When Mrs. Eddy decided to republish her articles from *The Christian Science Journal,* Mrs. Weller assisted by going through the *Journals,* clipping and pasting the articles onto paper, leaving wide margins on each page for Mrs. Eddy's revisions.

Working at the tailor shop, Mrs. Weller had learned the practical imperatives of obedience and precision: a cloth once cut could not be recut, coats and dresses had to fit — or time, effort, and supplies would be wasted. This was an exacting discipline, but a valuable one, one that she could bring to her study and practice of Christian Science. She also had the insight to perceive that the Discoverer and Founder of Christian Science had accepted the Christian discipline of self-sacrifice and obedience, as she wrote to Mrs. Eddy:

> *All that I know of God, good, has come to me through* your
> *self-sacrifice and obedience to Christian Science "the law of*
> *God." Your interpretation of Jesus' words and works* will
> *redeem the whole world. I* know *it and so do thousands*
> *of others.*[51]

On a memorable July Fourth in 1895, Mrs. Weller visited Mrs. Eddy at Pleasant View. After dinner the two retired to the library for a visit. Years later, Mrs. Weller would recall how firmly Mrs. Eddy had declared: "Christian Science is the last revelation that will ever come to humanity. It has come now in books, and is established in the world; and it can never be destroyed."[52] Although Mrs. Eddy might speak thus on one occasion to Janette Weller, she would also sound warnings, public and private, that the continuance of Christian Science among mankind rested upon demonstration, as when she wrote:

> *Comparing such students with those whose words are but*
> *the substitutes for works, we learn that the translucent*
> *atmosphere of the former must illumine the midnight of the*
> *latter, else Christian Science will disappear from among*
> *mortals.*[53]

Janette Weller was one of those people who expected her life to be measured by her works, rather than her words. Although she sometimes held strong opinions, she was devoted to Christian Science and loyal to Mrs. Eddy. During a time when Mrs. Eddy faced a particularly grave challenge — the "Next Friends" suit in 1907 — Mrs. Weller assured her: "I am writing a few lines to you, out of a heart full of love and gratitude for what you have done, are doing, and will continue to do, for me and all mankind." She continued:

> *I know it will give you a ray of comfort to be assured at this*
> *time, that in my twenty-three years' experience in Christian*
> *Science I have never for one moment doubted that you are*
> *God's messenger of truth to this age, and because you are His*
> *messenger, you cannot fail to fulfill your mission.*[54]

ANNIE MACMILLAN KNOTT

"ALL THE HOPES AND PRAYERS
OF THE EARLY YEARS HAD COME
TO A RESURRECTION MORN"

Annie Macmillan Knott, C.S.D., circa 1900.
Colorized photograph, private collection.

ANNIE MACMILLAN KNOTT

"ALL THE HOPES AND PRAYERS
OF THE EARLY YEARS HAD COME
TO A RESURRECTION MORN"

ANNIE MACMILLAN KNOTT HAD BEEN PRACTICING CHRISTIAN SCIENCE healing in Detroit, Michigan, about two years in 1887 when she was asked to take the case of a young man with dysentery. After diagnosing the disease in its most advanced stage, the doctor left the house, telling the parents their son, who had struggled with this for a year, now had twenty-four hours to live and probably would not even last another hour.[1]

Once Mrs. Knott took the case, a lot rested on its outcome.

Detroit newspapers were already on the attack against Christian Science and would certainly relish publishing pejorative news stories, were this man to pass away under the care of that city's pioneer Christian Scientist. That she was a student of Mary Baker Eddy, this new religion's Discoverer and Founder, would make her an even more tempting target.[2]

But Mrs. Knott, then in her mid-thirties, arrived at the house that day, confident she was bringing a very different verdict to this case. Indeed, a week earlier she had been sitting in Mary Baker Eddy's February 1887 Normal class, a teaching so powerful that Mrs. Knott reported a fundamental shift in her perspective.

"Mrs. Eddy's wonderful teaching in the recent class became so clear to me that I felt I could raise the dead if called upon to do so."[3] Writing of the effect of Mrs. Eddy's teaching, Mrs. Knott said: "She has taught us how to pray and to know that the answer is at hand awaiting our worthiness to receive it. She has taught us that Life is Good, and so we learn to live; and she is teaching us how to love since God is Love and God is all."[4]

The result of Mrs. Knott's work was that the man was healed — a healing that caused a stir in Detroit's medical community. When the original doctor on this case — one of Detroit's most respected physicians — came back to the house a few days later to visit the man's parents, he was startled to learn that the young man he had diagnosed as having twenty-four hours to live was now healthy.

The doctor said he could hardly believe this was the same man he had treated and began his own investigation of the facts of what had happened in this case, writing down what the parents told him about their son's healing in Christian Science. At a meeting of the Michigan Medical Association, this doctor reported in his findings that there had never been a case like this healed in the history of Michigan's medical practice, and that this healing was the result of Christian Science.[5]

"The dearest wish of my life"

IT WAS NO ACCIDENT THAT SCOTTISH-BORN, CANADIAN-RAISED, AMERICAN-immigrant Annie Knott found the path to Christian Science and its healing practice. Indeed, it was the inevitable result of Jesus' elegant equation: "Ask, and it shall be given you; seek, and ye shall find; knock, and it shall be opened unto you."[6]

Within the first decade since her birth in Scotland in 1850, the little Presbyterian girl, who had already committed whole chapters of the Bible to memory, was hoping that New Testament healing could be realized in the modern age.[7] The desire to help the sick ran so deep in her that it was one of the first facts she revealed about herself to Mrs. Eddy. "I may here say that since childhood almost the dearest wish of my life amounting almost to a passion was to be engaged in ministering to the sick," Mrs. Knott wrote in her first letter to Mrs. Eddy.[8]

This passion perhaps began in 1862 when a twelve-year-old Annie Macmillan went in earnest prayer to God to save the life of her eight-year-old sister, Mary, who was lying unconscious and near death at the Macmillan

Annie M. Knott as a young woman. Photograph, private collection.

family home in Ontario, Canada. Parents William and Catherine had given up hope of Mary's recovery.

From Annie's Presbyterian upbringing in Scotland, she had brought with her a deep love of the Bible and especially of Christ Jesus' healing of sickness. So, while others worried, Annie went to a private room in the house, kneeled down, and turned to God. She then returned to the room and looked down at her sister, who opened her eyes. "Do you know me, dear?" Annie asked her sister. Mary cheerily responded, "Of course I know you," and asked for something to eat.[9]

Annie decided not to tell anyone about her prayer for this healing, not even her parents. But she never forgot the lesson it taught her of the possibility of spiritual healing. It proved to be a powerful foundation block that had moved into place early in her life.

After her 1876 marriage to English-born Kennard Knott, the couple moved to England in 1878, where they spent four years. Mrs. Knott, then in her late twenties, volunteered at London-area hospitals, where she tended the sick. She did this even while she herself struggled with neuralgia, bronchitis, and other illnesses. She was also exploring alternative approaches to healing such as homeopathy, as Mrs. Eddy herself had done prior to her discovery of Christian Science.

"My mind was much occupied with metaphysical speculation," Mrs. Knott wrote of this period of her life, "for the nectar of life had turned to wormwood and gall in my personal experience."[10]

The gall Mrs. Knott mentioned included not only her own ill health but the death of a son in 1881, despite her employing a respected physician, Dr. Hahnemann, grandson of homeopathy founder, Samuel Hahnemann.[11] She would write that "the whole sad experience" prepared the way for her acceptance of Christian Science.

Another experience brought her to the brink of atheism. In London she attended an inspiring sermon by the noted Baptist preacher Charles Haddon Spurgeon[12] on Psalm 68:20: "He that is our God is the God of salvation; and unto God the Lord belong the issues from death." Deeply inspired by this sermon, she later had a private meeting with Spurgeon, only to be told that Christian healing was not possible in the modern age. This final, crushing disappointment from the great Spurgeon himself would, in her own words, have driven her into atheism, if she had not "caught a glimpse of Christian Science" as early as 1878.[13]

In January 1882 Mrs. Knott and two daughters, four-year-old Nellie (Helena Isabella born in 1877) and two-year-old Kate (born 1879), left England for the United States and rejoined her husband, who had moved to Chicago a year earlier. Here they added to the family a son, Frank.

It was in Chicago that the pivotal event of Mrs. Knott's life occurred — a desperate moment that forced her to turn wholeheartedly to God and Christian Science. At two o'clock one afternoon in 1884, Mrs. Knott heard her little son Frank's screams coming from the kitchen. When she entered the room, she discovered that her boy of just under two years old had swallowed a considerable amount of carbolic acid, a powerful disinfectant. Doctors arrived within a few minutes and called the case, at that stage of poisoning, utterly hopeless.

"The next half hour would be too painful to recall," Mrs. Knott wrote of this event, "were it not that it stands to-day in memory as the entrance into Life."[14]

Having heard about Christian Science from a Chicago friend who had been healed of a long-standing illness in just a few days, Mrs. Knott already owned and had been reading a copy of *Science and Health with Key to the Scriptures* by Mary Baker Eddy. With nowhere else to turn, she sought help from a Christian Science friend.

An absent treatment was given immediately to her son that resulted in quick relief from pain. The next morning a present treatment brought the complete healing. An hour later Frank found an apple in the pantry and ate it, thereby upending the doctor's prognosis that even if Frank survived, he would never again swallow normally.

The powerful healing that resulted that day not only saved her son's life but brought Mrs. Knott to the front door of her own life purpose.[15] "What words can tell the blessedness of that hour?" Mrs. Knott wrote of this healing. "It was not merely the child given back to life," she continued, "but all the hopes and prayers of the early years had come to a resurrection morn."[16] Some thirty years later she recalled, "I remembered and repeated to myself our Master's words, 'and if they drink any deadly thing, it shall not hurt them' (Mark 16:18).... To me it meant that Christian Science had come to restore to us all that our Master had promised...."[17]

Humbled and in deep gratitude, Mrs. Knott began a focused study of *Science and Health*. "What a revelation it brought!" she wrote. "Day by day its teaching opened up to me the long-hidden riches of the word of God, through which all may hold communion with prophets, apostles, and saints, and sit at the feet of our Lord and Master and be made whole."[18]

As she studied, Mrs. Knott found herself being healed of the long-standing neuralgia and bronchitis.

As with many of the other early Christian Science pioneers, after she was healed, Mrs. Knott started to help and heal others simply by applying the truths she was learning from *Science and Health*. To her amazement, she reported having great success "in every case."[19]

The healing of her son sent Mrs. Knott onto a new life-path that turned into a nearly sixty-year labor of love for others until her passing at ninety-one in December 1941. She would serve the Christian Science movement as practitioner, teacher, pastor and preacher, First Reader, lecturer, Sunday School teacher, Associate Editor of the Christian Science periodicals, member of the Bible Lesson Committee, and the first woman member of the Christian Science Board of Directors.

Mrs. Knott's healing work in Detroit flowed from a single focus of energy and commitment to Christian Science. Indeed, Mrs. Knott's private papers, letters, and reminiscences reveal a woman who set out to master the discipline of discipleship — in a word, obedience — so she could fulfill her lifelong desire to bring healing and comfort to the sick. As Mrs. Knott wrote, "Every step taken in obedience to divine law means far more than we are able to see at the time, or, perhaps, for long years thereafter."[20]

With this as her approach, Mrs. Knott's Christianity was set firmly on the pavement of life, and through it she learned how to surrender her weaknesses, fears, and inabilities in order to discover her God-derived power and dominion.

Here lay the secret of Mrs. Knott's success.

It would earn her the affection and respect of Mrs. Eddy.

It would earn her great admiration from the early Christian Science community.

Today, the name Annie Macmillan Knott is among the most esteemed of the Christian Science pioneers.

"The cry of my whole nature is 'more light'"

WITH THE RELIEF AND JOY OF HER SON'S HEALING, THE CENTRAL FOCUS of Mrs. Knott's life during the 1880s was to gain a deeper understanding of Christian Science through studying Mrs. Eddy's writings. During this decade she would also take three courses in Christian Science: Primary class with Bradford Sherman in 1884,[21] and in 1887 and 1888 the Normal and Obstetrics classes with Mary Baker Eddy.

"The cry of my whole nature is 'more light,'" Mrs. Knott wrote Mrs. Eddy in an 1888 letter summarizing this period of her life.[22]

While she was still living in Chicago and just beginning to take patients, her husband abandoned her and their children. Before her marriage she had spent some time in Detroit and had friends there, so it was natural for her to relocate to that city. She arrived in Detroit in March 1885 and began to introduce

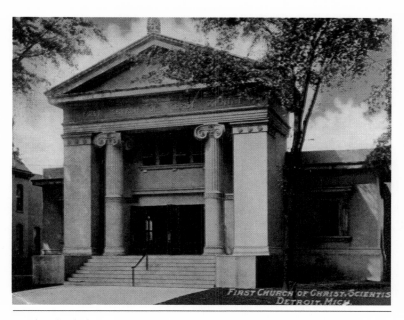

First Church of Christ, Scientist, Detroit, Michigan. Colorized postcard, circa 1910, Longyear Museum Collection.

Christian Science, remaining there for eighteen years, until Mrs. Eddy called her to Boston in 1903. She built up a large healing practice, taught classes in Christian Science, and helped establish Detroit's First Church of Christ, Scientist.

In her pursuit of more light, Mrs. Knott became a student in Mrs. Eddy's Normal class of February 1887. The events that took place on that first day of class would linger in Mrs. Knott's memory throughout her life. Not only would she meet Mrs. Eddy for the first time, but she would be healed at that first meeting of painfully cold hands, a condition to which she had been susceptible since childhood.

Mrs. Knott arrived at the Massachusetts Metaphysical College for the first day of what would be a six-day class. Extreme winter temperatures, a long walk to the College, and forgetting to bring her hand-warming muff had made Mrs. Knott's hands red and painful. Mrs. Eddy warmly greeted her new student, taking her hands into her own and asking whether she were cold.

Proceeding to the classroom, Mrs. Knott noticed her hands were now warm, the discomfort had vanished, as had the redness and roughness. She had been healed.[23]

Years later, as this story was retold among Christian Scientists, this healing would be distorted and exaggerated, and the condition of Mrs. Knott's hands came to be described as chapped, raw, and bleeding. Mrs. Knott said that in consequence she would receive letters from people requesting her to heal their chapped hands, believing it was the same condition that Mrs. Eddy had healed. This experience also may have contributed to her sensitivities to the importance of having healings attributed to Mary Baker Eddy properly attested.[24]

Mrs. Knott would take home many important lessons from this class, but what took place on the fifth day would prove startling. The subject was malicious animal magnetism. As Mrs. Eddy began teaching on this subject, the whole atmosphere of the classroom changed. She grew stern as she warned her students that they were not sufficiently recognizing this error and that unless they did awaken to it and prove its nothingness, they would be made to hate her:

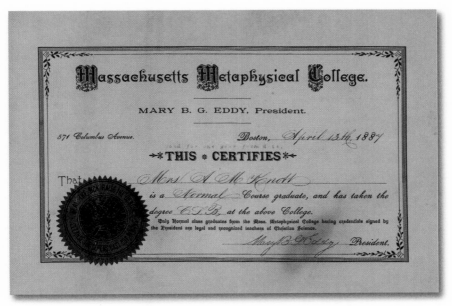

Annie M. Knott's Normal Course certificate from the Massachusetts Metaphysical College in Boston, 1887, private collection.

It was indeed painful to most of us to be told that if we yielded in the least to the arguments of animal magnetism every one of us would come to hate her, and we would thus be led away from Christian Science. She then gave instances of students who had gone astray in this way and who had left the Science.[25]

Mrs. Eddy continued to take the class to a point of intensity Mrs. Knott found challenging: "Mrs. Eddy…in her mental surgery went deeper and deeper until some of us wondered if we would be able to stand by the truth and our Leader, and defend this great Cause which had come to save the whole world from sickness, sin, and death."[26]

At the end of this class session, Mrs. Eddy's assistant, Calvin Frye, copied and handed out to each student a statement by Mrs. Eddy on this subject. The document read:

In treating against malpractice the student must not call the names of individuals because he cannot know who is sinning always but he can make sin to himself nothing through divine Science. Declare positively, mortal minds cannot harm me or my patients. One Mind governs all harmoniously.[27]

A year and a half later, a conversation showed Mrs. Knott something of what Mrs. Eddy herself had to contend with. Mrs. Eddy asked Mrs. Knott to run an errand with fellow Christian Science worker Julia Bartlett. As the two went about their errand, their conversation turned to what had taken place a few months earlier: a group of about fifty "mental scientists" had sent word to Mrs. Eddy that that night they were going to mentally kill her. After listening to Miss Bartlett's account, Mrs. Knott remarked that Mrs. Eddy would "pay no attention to that."

Miss Bartlett replied: "I spent the whole of that night with Mrs. Eddy and I know what Gethsemane means."[28]

Miss Bartlett's statement carried the power of a hammer blow as Mrs. Knott came to realize more fully the cost Mrs. Eddy was paying to establish Christian Science. The incident also served as an element of initiation, bringing Mrs. Knott deeper into the inner realm where Mrs. Eddy lived and worked with a small group of intensely loyal followers who themselves were paying their dues — living their lives on call to further Mrs. Eddy's mission. "I never said anything like that again, nor did I think that way," Mrs. Knott wrote of this incident.[29]

"I know you are doing great good"

WITH THE CLASS OVER AND ANNIE KNOTT BACK IN HER DETROIT HOME, SHE was called to the case of a man whose violent insanity demanded that three attendants hold him down. For her own safety she was not allowed into his room, but from a small room nearby she prayed for him for about a half-hour. The moment she began her work, the man became "calm and peaceful." He

Mary Macmillan, sister of Annie M. Knott.
Photograph, Tomlinson, Detroit, circa 1880, private collection.

then talked to his son and wife perfectly normally. The guards were dismissed. One additional treatment the next day completed the healing, and years later Mrs. Knott saw this man attending her branch church on Sundays.

By the summer of 1887, Mrs. Knott, with the assistance of her sister Mary (the sister she had healed as a little girl), had opened the Detroit Christian Science Institute. The letterhead of the sisters' new stationery detailed the particulars of the enterprise: A. M. Knott, C.S.B., Principal, Normal class graduate of Mass. Metaphysical College, and M. Macmillan, C.S.B., Assistant, 115 Miami Ave., Detroit, Mich.[30]

Mrs. Knott's healing work gained attention from the late 1880s, perhaps because, as she once told Mrs. Eddy, the healings occurred "quickly." She also noticed that from the time of her classes with Mrs. Eddy, the cases that were now coming to her for help were much more difficult than those of her first two years of practice, and were resulting in remarkable outcomes that could sometimes surprise even her. "I was even astonished at the results in these cases," she said.[31]

Mrs. Eddy was aware of Mrs. Knott's early efforts and sent letters of support and encouragement: "I know you are doing great good and God is with you alway," Mrs. Eddy wrote her on March 19, 1887,[32] and the following year admonished her: "Press on we are a Unit in love and I rejoice over the good you are doing and will do."[33]

In fact, Mrs. Knott *was* doing great good.

When a Mrs. Webster visiting from Tilton, New Hampshire, came to Mrs. Knott with a severe illness, the practitioner agreed to take the case, despite the woman's proud admission that she had a negative opinion of Mrs. Eddy, had no interest in Christian Science, and no faith that it could heal her.

Mrs. Knott retorted: "I would not care two cents for your faith."

When a surprised Mrs. Webster asked her why, Mrs. Knott answered: "Because you do not know anything about God and Christian Science."[34]

As she began to pray, her patient issued a revision of her former statement. "It is extraordinary, but I believe, Mrs. Knott, that I can be healed in Christian Science," Mrs. Webster said. "I have the most wonderful faith that Christian Science can heal the sick."

The next morning Mrs. Webster found herself completely healed. She ate her first normal meal in a long while. Mrs. Knott received many new patients who heard of Mrs. Webster's healing and decided to investigate Christian Science.[35]

But even as Mrs. Knott was finding early success in Detroit, she was fully aware that the practice of Christian Science was not legally protected. Her sister and brother-in-law Isabella M. and John H. Stewart of Toronto were charged with the unlawful practice of medicine and were threatened with fines and imprisonment. Mrs. Knott informed Mrs. Eddy of the legal challenges her sister and brother-in-law were facing: "They have again and again, been dragged before magistrates and fined heavily and while their appeals were pending in the Superior Court, they were, contrary to all law and precedent, brought up again.... My sister Mrs. Stewart was [brought] before a magistrate and sentenced to pay 75 dollars and costs, or go to prison for three months.... Last week, however, the chief justice gave a decision in favor of our cause."[36]

Isabella M. Stewart, C.S.D., (sister of Annie M. Knott) and John H. Stewart, C.S.B.
Photograph, Charles J. Neil, Toronto, Ontario, Longyear Museum Collection.

"I read thought usually as easily as a book"

AT THIS PERIOD IN THE DEVELOPMENT OF HER HEALING PRACTICE, ANNIE Knott found that her cases were not only more demanding, but also involved more subtle, hidden error. Even as she was increasingly demonstrating that "Truth does the work,"[37] she was also seeing that Truth would uncover whatever needed healing.

One such case was that of a young woman. Mrs. Knott arrived at the house and was told the illness was a severe bilious case, possibly appendicitis. But as she began to treat her patient, Mrs. Knott sensed something was being hidden from her. "I quickly saw that it was a case of abortion, and after giving faithful treatment the patient admitted that this was the case and expressed her regret for the moral error which had led her to take this step," Mrs. Knott wrote. She requested her patient to tell her mother what had taken place and a short time later the healing was complete.[38]

Local newspaper articles at that time had reported on many illegal abortions being performed. Patients were dying as a result, and these backroom abortion doctors were often being prosecuted. Mrs. Knott had a few cases of this type and quickly discerned the hidden error.

In another situation a student, believing that her young child had a sore throat, brought the child to Mrs. Knott, who decided to keep both mother and child close for an hour. After the work began, Mrs. Knott sensed the child had swallowed an object. At that point she allowed them to go home and did not inform the mother of her suspicion that the child had swallowed something, but found herself having to deal with the suggestion that an operation might be necessary to correct the problem. She continued her metaphysical treatment, however, and two hours later received word from the mother saying the child had passed a penny and all was well.

Spiritual intuition and moral courage guided Mrs. Knott's practice. In 1895 she wrote to Mrs. Eddy: "I read thought usually as easily as a book, and with my patients seldom fail to bring out good results...."[39]

One day she felt impelled to visit a former patient whom she had previously healed. She arrived at the house only to discover the woman was unconscious, and a doctor in attendance said the patient would not live through the day. Mrs. Knott demanded that she be allowed to see her former patient and began at once to pray. As in the case of the child who swallowed a penny, Mrs. Knott in this situation had an intuition that the case involved a toxic substance, although she did not tell this to anyone.

"I was fully convinced that it was a case of poisoning and that it might have been accidental, but I did not even hint of this to anyone," Mrs. Knott wrote. "The patient responded quickly to the treatment, and when I reached her room [the patient] was able to speak, and although a trained nurse was there, she begged me for treatment...." The woman was healed and became a Christian Scientist.[40]

"It may be said that hundreds have been healed whose cases had been pronounced incurable by medical doctors," Annie Knott wrote in her letter for Detroit's "Century Box" (a sealed box containing over fifty letters that would be opened in one hundred years). She added:

> ... *in every case these persons have had the moral nature quickened, the mental faculties set free to master the problem of man's high destiny, — and the infinite possibilities of spiritual Being at least awakened, and recognized as the source of all real progression toward the sublime end of existence, — even the unfoldment of man's likeness to God.*[41]

Sometimes the healings not only reversed the dire medical predictions; they also touched the lives of those who witnessed the healings, setting them on a new path. A Detroit woman had given birth to two children, each with a birth defect and each passing away a year after birth. When the mother found herself pregnant again, her doctor urged her to have an abortion. Instead, she called Mrs. Knott for help. Undaunted by the medical predictions, Mrs. Knott took the case: "I... did not hesitate to treat the mother, and urged her to study in the Bible the one perfect human character, that of Christ Jesus."

Six months later, a healthy child was born. Mrs. Knott reported that, despite her hopes after this success, the parents showed no interest in Christian Science, although some of their relatives who heard of this healing *did* take it up.[42]

"This brave just defense of Christian Science"

"IT REQUIRES COURAGE TO UTTER TRUTH," WROTE THE DISCOVERER AND Founder of Christian Science, adding, "for the higher Truth lifts her voice, the louder will error scream, until its inarticulate sound is forever silenced in oblivion."[43]

Late one night during the winter of 1896–97, Mrs. Knott sat in the Michigan Capitol in Lansing listening intently to the Committee of the Whole debate a bill that would have restricted the practice of Christian Science. Hearing Mary Baker Eddy's teachings sorely misrepresented, Mrs. Knott requested permission to speak against the bill.

She had not intended to speak, had made no preparation to do so, and now on the spur of the moment, this loyal practitioner requested ten minutes to address the audience that included hostile professionals with formidable credentials.

"I had to go out in the corridor and declare the truth," Mrs. Knott later recalled. "I thought I should faint when they asked me…. The speakers were all university professors and leading doctors speaking before all evening."[44]

Praying for wisdom, she began her talk by identifying herself as "a student of the author of *Science and Health*." She related the stories of several recent smallpox cases, two that had been treated through Christian Science and two that had chosen medicine. The two that chose Christian Science had both been healed. She related that of the two under medical care, one had passed on and the other had a difficult time but recovered. She concluded her remarks as the clock struck midnight.

"I had the closest attention from all present," she wrote Mrs. Eddy on May 7, and "made a strong plea for the great moral and spiritual power of C.S. — as well as its wonderful healing of the body."[45]

It would be several months before the issue was resolved, but during the final debate on May 5, the chairman of the House Committee, a medical doctor himself, announced that "all the powers of earth and hell cannot [stop the practice of Christian Science] as it is a religious belief," as a grateful Annie Knott wrote in her May 7 letter to Mrs. Eddy.

> *We have had a signal victory in the state legislature over a medical bill. It has been a long hard fight and the bill has passed — but by an amendment strongly contested declares Christian Scientists exempt from its provisions.*[46]

Mrs. Eddy at once replied: " 'Scots wha hae wi' Wallace bled' — have a moral force innate. Thank God, and my faithful Annie for this brave just defense of Christian Science."[47]

"Will you *do* it?"

IN HER HIGHLY SUCCESSFUL HEALING PRACTICE, MRS. KNOTT OBSERVED THAT
although patients could leave her office healed, they would then return to their
own denominational churches, where they again listened to sermons on
the nature of man as being material, his fall from grace, and his everlasting
punishment. These patients would then need to return to Mrs. Knott for
more help.[48]

"Those healed remained in their old churches because we had, of course,
not a church of our own to which we could invite them," Mrs. Knott wrote,
"consequently those who were healed made little or no progress.... It was more
and more clearly seen that Christian Science churches alone could establish
and maintain the Christ healing."[49]

Mrs. Knott once made this very point to her friend and fellow pioneer
Christian Scientist Abigail Dyer Thompson, calling these patients who had
been healed "precious beads" that rolled away. A Christian Science church, Mrs.
Knott told her friend, was like a piece of string that brought all these beads
together, providing structure and connection.

That the time had come for Churches of Christ, Scientist, to be established
was a topic of a lengthy private meeting in October 1888 between Mrs. Eddy
and Mrs. Knott. In Detroit, she had already been holding informal Sunday
services in her home for her own students; now Mrs. Eddy directed her to
begin holding public services.

To help prepare Mrs. Knott for preaching, Mrs. Eddy requested her to
obtain several standard books on biblical topics, in particular: *Notes on the
Miracles of Our Lord* and *Notes on the Parables of Our Lord,* both by Richard
Chenevix Trench (Anglican Archbishop of Dublin); *The Life and Epistles of
the Apostle Paul* by W. J. Conybeare and J. S. Howson (two noted Anglican cler-
gymen); and *The History of Christianity* by John S. C. Abbott.[50]

At the end of the interview Mrs. Eddy wanted to know for certain that
Mrs. Knott would carry out her orders to hold public worship. She asked her
if she would obey. When Mrs. Knott answered that she would try, Mrs. Eddy

Clergyman's Order for Half Fare rate on train
travel, issued to Annie M. Knott, 1895,
private collection.

told her the answer was not enough.

"Will you *do* it?" Mrs. Eddy asked her.

"Yes!" Mrs. Knott answered.

"Then, do not forget!" Mrs. Eddy responded.[51]

Struggling in her early years with a fear of public speaking, Mrs. Knott once let her imagination run wild in a kind of "worst case" scenario: "The first time you tried that, you would probably be carried out on a shutter before the service was over."[52] Working to heal this, she obeyed Mrs. Eddy and began public services in her house, while suitable Detroit locations for a church were being scouted.

"We held our first Sunday Service in my house last Sabbath," she wrote Mrs. Eddy in December 1888. "I read Gen. 21st — the story of Hagar. I began by quoting from Science and Health the old edition 'There is neither personal deity, personal devil, nor personal man.'. . . I dwelt upon the thought of womanhood, not one personal woman as believed in by mortal mind. The subject appeared to me infinitely suggestive. The opening of Hagar's eyes, as spiritual discernment whereby the good always existing, but unseen because of the sense of error, was appropriated and understood, has so much in it."[53]

This congregation in Detroit continued to prosper. Nine months later,

Mrs. Knott reported they had held their first Sunday service in a public location, Royal Templar Hall (also known as Barnes Hall), in September 1889. Seven years later, First Church of Christ, Scientist, Detroit, was thriving, as Mrs. Knott informed Mrs. Eddy in a May 1896 letter: "Our church prospers greatly, — and chiefly in the growing recognition and admission that the Church of Christ, Scientist, is nearest to the teachings of the great Master."[54]

First Church of Christ, Scientist, Detroit, was incorporated on May 3, 1897,[55] and early the following year the branch took possession of a building in the "best residence part of the city."[56]

This first Christian Science church building in Michigan was dedicated on Sunday, February 13, 1898, with Mrs. Knott presiding as First Reader at the three services. The April *Journal* proclaimed: "A fine new church edifice was dedicated" — debt-free and with a thousand dollars remaining in the church building fund.[57] Three years later the congregation would number three hundred.[58]

In her dedicatory address, Mrs. Knott spoke of those who had come out of the darkness and into the light according to prophecy:

> *In St. John's wonderful vision, we are told of a great multitude which no man could number, standing before the throne, and the beloved disciple tells us, that they all came out of great tribulation.*

She undoubtedly drew from her own experience in the next paragraph:

> *And this is the chief characteristic of Christian Science churches, that the members have come from the depths of human woe, mental and physical, in most cases where hope and faith were faltering and failing, and have found in this great revelation, what? even the fulfilling of every word of prophecy, not only the prophecy written in the Bible, but the promise and prophecy of every individual life and hope, the fulfilling of God's good pleasure in us.*[59]

Mrs. Eddy telegraphed Annie Knott and the Detroit church:

> Beloved Students and Church: — *Thanks for invitation to your dedication. Not afar off I am blending with thine my prayer and rejoicing. God is with thee. "Arise, shine; for thy light is come, and the glory of the Lord is risen upon thee."*[60]

"Perception, Reception, Conception"

MRS. KNOTT'S SECOND AND FINAL CLASS WITH MRS. EDDY WOULD BE the Obstetrics course of October 1888. A few weeks before this class began, Mrs. Knott seemed to sense her need for this advanced teaching, writing Mrs. Eddy on September 10 with this new and broader definition of obstetrics: "In our work of late it has come to us in a very striking way how the obstetrics of Christian Science is needed for every one coming to us for treatment, that the Divine idea may be conceived and born in human consciousness."[61]

In her teaching of obstetrics, Mrs. Eddy "endeavored to lift thought above mortal sense," Mrs. Knott wrote, "and used the following terms to present the unfoldment of the spiritual idea along mental and spiritual lines, namely, — Perception, Reception, Conception." Mrs. Knott recalled:

> *Although her students were slow in grasping her meaning, nevertheless she patiently worked on until we could see how spiritual ideals would displace all mortal beliefs about being. She made it clear that perception of the truth must come first to the individual, then the next step must of necessity be its reception before progress could be made, and this led to the conception of the divine idea of which St. Paul speaks when he says: "My little children, of whom I travail in birth again until Christ be formed in you" (Gal. 4:19).*[62]

"Returning good for evil makes good real and evil unreal"

ANNIE KNOTT'S LOVE FOR MRS. EDDY WAS NOT PERSONAL WORSHIP. IT WAS a consecration and devotion to Mrs. Eddy's purpose as the Discoverer and Founder of Christian Science. While her love for her teacher was boundless, her focus was on demonstrating the truth Mrs. Eddy had revealed.

As a result, Mrs. Knott rarely went to Mrs. Eddy for personal help. On a few occasions, in moments of great need, she did ask for guidance, but her primary concern was not to burden Mrs. Eddy. For Mrs. Knott, the test of Christian Scientists' love for their Leader was their willingness to obey what *Science and Health* and the *Church Manual* demanded. In these two books, Mrs. Eddy provided the student with the guidance necessary to succeed.

"When we love God and our Leader well enough to obey whole-heartedly the provisions of the Manual," Mrs. Knott said in a 1921 address, "we shall know beyond any question that its provisions are of God, not only for our need today, but for all human needs, making the establishment of God's kingdom on earth possible."[63]

In an editorial entitled "The Study of the Manual," Mrs. Knott explored this idea, showing how the rules, though they might appear confining to the human mind, contain the path to success:

> *The purpose of all the rules contained in the Manual is to aid Christian Scientists in becoming "a law unto themselves,"*
> *— a condition indispensable to the establishment of true democracy alike in Church and State. In Christian Science we come to understand the inherent goodness of divine law, even if, to mortal sense, its provisions seem restrictive. To the Truth-enlightened thought it means liberty and progress. The study of the Manual also aids us in apprehending and applying to present conditions the infinite provisions of this spiritual law so as to benefit others as well as ourselves.*[64]

Mrs. Knott was always looking for ways to support Mrs. Eddy and her mission. Sometimes that meant sending an encouraging letter at the right moment. After a sensational newspaper attack on Mrs. Eddy in 1906, Mrs. Knott's letter of support deeply touched Mrs. Eddy.

"Your excellent letter like the morning ray shone on the clouds," Mrs. Eddy wrote Mrs. Knott. "I *Thank* you. Evil is venting itself, and when found out will have done with itself what needs to be done, fallen not to rise again. God is One and *All* — God is good — is Love and this reassures us. So we toil on and await the results watching in faith, hope, love. Returning good for evil makes good real and evil unreal. God bless you dear, with all that blesses."[65]

"What I desire is a clear sense above mortal belief"

MRS. KNOTT'S EARLY SUCCESS ENCOUNTERED A PERIOD OF TRIAL BY FIRE IN the mid-1890s. From this series of events that might have upended the commitment of a halfhearted hireling, Mrs. Knott would emerge stronger and more certain of God's power than ever before.

From the time she took Mrs. Eddy's Obstetrics course, she began to see the importance of going on the offensive against error, rather than waiting for it to present itself. She had observed Mrs. Eddy's proactive dealing with mortal mind, and mentioned this in a talk she gave forty years later in 1928 — a talk that was rich in the perspective gained from hard-won battles and severe challenges:

> *I had been learning the great lesson that we cannot afford to ignore the threats of mortal mind, that we must face them bravely, no matter what the cost may be to us in the way of suffering. Our Leader was awake and alert and sometimes there was a severe sense of suffering which had to be overcome, yet we must never lose sight of the fact that through her untiring work our Cause was saved and will be if we are as faithful as was our Master and as was our Leader.*[66]

The challenging events that confronted Mrs. Knott in the mid-1890s included the startling discovery that several of her students had been deceiving her. Worse yet, she learned that they were attempting mentally to make her believe that she was mistaken in her uncovering of their deception. One student confessed to her this mental intrusion and promised to reform but failed to do so. Mrs. Knott found these students stubbornly resistant to reformation and moral growth. In 1894, while this crisis was still raging, her forty-year-old sister Mary Macmillan passed away — the sister whom she had healed as a little girl and who had worked with her in the Detroit Christian Science Institute from its inception.

As the challenge from a few of her students continued, Mrs. Knott wrote her teacher an anguished letter in the summer of 1895:

> *Now my dear Teacher, I have never in all my years of work intruded upon you any of my difficulties.... What I desire is a clear sense above mortal belief — that I may not merely uncover, — but destroy the error.*[67]

After another severe struggle, she wrote her teacher the following May that she had "sounded the depths of Science, and grown stronger and better, — I trust!"[68]

But ten days later Mrs. Knott would face a new depth, when her beloved nineteen-year-old daughter Nellie passed on. "In spite of all I could do," she wrote Mrs. Eddy, "my darling and I parted, though I am sure only for 'a little while'":

> *The wild waves of sorrow swept over me, but only to make me realize more than ever the solid rock beneath my feet, and with the peace of Christ I was able to lift higher than ever the sense of my students....*
>
> *My daughter was the dearest of all on earth to me, so sweet and fair, caring only to share my cares and trials — loyally and truly devoted to our great cause.*[69]

Mrs. Eddy's heartfelt response was a remarkable letter of both comfort and power, stating a promise of what was possible:

> *Well dear one, you have no cause to doubt God's love for you and your child. And if He loves you He doeth all things that is for your good. But He does not destroy the work of His hands. You alone and all mortals are responsible for mortal conditions. They make them and they yield them up. Why do they give up what is so dear to them? Because they know not yet how to retain them as reality.*
>
> *Therefore wait on God and Love will teach you how and do not mourn over the lessons of Love but rejoice. For Love knows best and you and I wait to learn what is best.*[70]

Mrs. Eddy signed this letter "Lovingly thine in sorrow or in joy Mother, M B Eddy."

Mrs. Knott had a typed duplicate of this letter, to which she added and initialed the poignant comment: "This I value more than any other. A. M. K."

"Sorrow has its reward," Mary Baker Eddy writes in *Science and Health*. "It never leaves us where it found us."[71] Mrs. Knott would take much from such bitter lessons, finding herself able to help others see more clearly the spiritual nature of true relationship.[72] Sentences such as the following from a 1905 editorial emerge molten from the crucible of suffering, take form on the anvil of spiritual growth, and are burnished by the desire to make the paths of others brighter:

> *We should not overlook the fact that so long as we regard anything, or any relation of life, materially, we shall be subject to varying phases of discord, until every affection, motive, and endeavor is spiritualized, and we see things as they are in God's sight.*[73]

Calls to higher duties

THE YEAR 1898 MARKED A WATERSHED IN MRS. KNOTT'S WORK AND CAREER AS a Christian Scientist. Up to that time, her primary focus had been on gaining an understanding of Christian Science and demonstrating what she had learned by healing the sick and sinning. By 1898 her practice was thriving, and she was busy teaching classes and tending to the needs of her student association.

In this critical year Mary Baker Eddy was taking measures to strengthen the Christian Science movement: she established the Board of Lectureship; created The Christian Science Publishing Society in its present form; designated the topics for the Lesson-Sermons; launched the weekly religious periodical *Christian Science Sentinel;* taught her last class; and took steps to create the Committee on Publication.

In June Mrs. Eddy requested that Mrs. Knott join the Board of Lectureship. This proved to be the first in a series of appointments that would propel Mrs. Knott from her singular focus on her beloved Detroit vineyard into "a wider sphere of thought and action."[74] Five years later she would be called to Boston by Mrs. Eddy to become an assistant editor of the periodicals. A year after, Mrs. Eddy assigned her two additional posts: member of the Bible Lesson Committee and Sunday School teacher, where she taught college-age women in The Mother Church. Fifteen years after that, she would become a Director of The First Church of Christ, Scientist. Just as her healing work had proved a laboratory for demonstration, she recognized that these new duties were also laboratories demanding that Christian Science be demonstrated at every step.

The July issue of the *Journal* announced the appointment of the first two women to serve as lecturers: Annie M. Knott and Sue Harper Mims. Mrs. Knott and Edward Kimball were assigned the lecture territory of the middle and western part of the United States, from Michigan to, but not including, the states along the Pacific Coast.

Mrs. Eddy spoke to her on the subject of lecturing, and Mrs. Knott found herself drawing on Mrs. Eddy's wisdom soon thereafter. Mrs. Eddy indicated that she should prepare her lectures "carefully," submit a copy to the Board of Directors, and yet be flexible enough to address the unique needs that might arise in a specific moment in the lecture hall.

"You must look for your inspiration in what God gives you at the time," Mrs. Eddy told her, "not in what is manufactured."[75]

Fairly new to this activity, Mrs. Knott began a lecture on Christian Science one evening in Salt Lake City, unaware that sitting in the audience was a hypnotist intent on throwing her off-track. The hypnotist had come to Salt Lake City to teach a class on how to control people's thinking. After learning that a Christian Science lecturer (Mrs. Knott) was in town to speak, he decided to cancel his scheduled class and attend the lecture instead, to make it an object-lesson in mental manipulation for his students.

Although Mrs. Knott had been told a hypnotist was in town, she knew nothing of his plan to target her specifically. But as she spiritually prepared for this lecture, she felt "somewhat troubled." However, once the lecture was under way she had a "marvelous illumination," and, obeying Mrs. Eddy's admonition to rely on divine guidance, she departed from her prepared remarks and discussed the difference between Christian Science and hypnotism.

"I never before had given a lecture with such a wonderful sense of freedom," Mrs. Knott wrote about this lecture, "and when I returned to the room where I was staying I wrote down what I could remember of my own remarks, the strong point being the one divine Mind as ever present."[76]

It would be several months before Mrs. Knott would discover the full story behind what had taken place that night. The person who revealed the story to Mrs. Knott had been in Salt Lake City that night and knew a student of this hypnotist. The hypnotist had told those interested in learning hypnotism that if they attended the Christian Science lecture that evening they could witness him knock the lecturer off her track.

"She would most likely become so confused that she would hardly know her own name if asked," this hypnotist was reported to have said.[77]

But when he came into the hall and tried to disorient Mrs. Knott, he quickly realized he was getting nowhere. He later explained to his students that someone must have tipped the lecturer off to his plan. The fact was, Mrs. Knott was unaware that he would attend her lecture. She later observed that if she had been told, she might have been troubled. "But when the adverse mental influence was felt," Mrs. Knott wrote, "I never before had been so clear, for it was as if God was telling me how to defend our Cause, and for months, in all the work which followed, this remarkable illumination was with me to a large extent."[78]

Early in her lecture work, Mrs. Knott found herself with few requests to lecture — a fact she shared with Mrs. Eddy at a January 1899 meeting at Pleasant View. People preferred men as lecturers, Mrs. Knott told her. Mrs. Knott was hearing this even from her own Christian Science friends.

Mrs. Eddy refused to let that argument stand. She told Mrs. Knott in no uncertain terms it was her responsibility to make her lecturing work a matter of Christian Science demonstration. "You must rise to the altitude of true womanhood," Mrs. Eddy told her, "and then the whole world will want you as it wants Mother."[79]

Mrs. Knott came away from the conversation with a new understanding, and within a short period of time she was busy lecturing to large and appreciative crowds. One woman, a former Lutheran, who heard Mrs. Knott lecture to a standing-room-only audience in February 1899, reported the revelation that came to her: "I never understood the unreality of evil so clearly before," she said, as quoted in the *Sheboygan* [Wisconsin] *Daily Journal*. Said another audience member, "That woman would win a heart of stone, for she denounced nothing but simply filled the void of human craving with hope and divine Love." Many of those who had stood said that if Mrs. Knott had spoken longer, they would gladly have remained standing for another hour.[80]

A notebook kept by Mrs. Knott records her leaving Detroit on April 11, 1899, to lecture in Kansas City, Missouri; then on to Ardmore, Oklahoma, on April 13; then to Dallas, Texas, and on April 21 to San Antonio; then on to Marshall, Texas, and to Parsons, Kansas; back to Kansas City (probably for a second lecture), Topeka and Riley, Kansas; back again to Marshall, Texas;

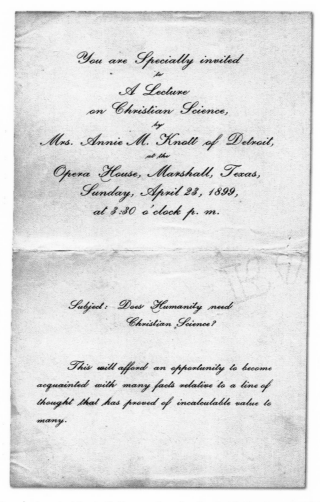

You are Specially invited
to
A Lecture
on Christian Science,
by
Mrs. Annie M. Knott of Detroit,
at the
Opera House, Marshall, Texas,
Sunday, April 23, 1899,
at 3:30 o'clock p. m.

Subject: Does Humanity need
Christian Science?

This will afford an opportunity to become
acquainted with many facts relative to a line of
thought that has proved of incalculable value to
many.

Invitation to a lecture in Marshall, Texas, given by Annie M. Knott on April 23, 1899, private collection.

then to Seneca, Atchison, and Beloit, Kansas; and finally on to St. Louis, Minneapolis, and Elkhart, Indiana.[81]

"She will earn it"

ABOUT THE BEGINNING OF JUNE 1903, MRS. KNOTT RECEIVED A TELEGRAM FROM
William B. Johnson, Clerk of The Mother Church, requesting her to come to his
office the following Monday morning. At their meeting, he informed her that at
Mrs. Eddy's request she had been appointed assistant editor of *The Christian
Science Journal* and *Christian Science Sentinel*. Her duties would include writing
a monthly editorial for the *Journal* and a weekly editorial for the *Sentinel*; review-
ing and editing articles and testimonies submitted for publication; examining
proof pages; and carrying out whatever correspondence was necessary.

Accepting the position, she learned a short while later that her salary was to
be quite small. She brought the matter up with William P. McKenzie, a trustee of
The Christian Science Publishing Society, who told her that her salary was out
of his hands, as it was determined by the Board of Directors and Mrs. Eddy.
Mrs. Knott requested an annual salary of $2,500[82] — a not insignificant sum,
given that a United States Senator at that time made $5,000. It should be noted,
however, that Mrs. Knott anticipated (correctly) that she would have to give up
her teaching, thus losing an annual income of up to three thousand dollars, in
addition to her income from lecturing.[83]

Mrs. Eddy had a straightforward response to Mrs. Knott's salary request:
Pay it! "It is just to pay Mrs. Knott her price and she will earn it I trust,"
Mrs. Eddy wrote, observing that she was "good, well educated" and noting that
Mrs. Knott had been under her personal instruction:

> A student qualified thus the Directors know is needed on the
> staff editorial. Do not fail to secure her price and so inform
> her at once.[84]

Mrs. Knott accepted the position and in ten days was in Boston, had found
a place to live, written her first editorial, and then returned temporarily to
Detroit to tend to some matters there.

Mrs. Knott did indeed earn her salary. For starters, the move demanded
that she leave everything she had spent over a decade and a half building — a

beloved home, friends, a thriving Christian Science healing practice, and teaching Christian Science.

It proved a wrenching change. "I was very unhappy for a few days," Mrs. Knott wrote of this period, "but I worked earnestly to overcome that sense...."[85]

Several weeks after Mrs. Knott's arrival, Mrs. Eddy's plans for her to visit Pleasant View were already under way. "I long to see you and have a chat as of old with one of my tried and true students."[86]

Two months later, Mrs. Eddy was busy but still hoping for that visit: "When, O when shall I have one hour with you!"[87] The hour did in fact come and stretched into a visit of a few days, Mrs. Knott noting that she treasured every minute with her teacher.[88]

Once in her new job as Associate Editor, Mrs. Knott found she enjoyed this challenging work. She would write nearly a thousand editorials, in her unique voice and with insights that readers came to expect.

Mrs. Knott's sometimes complex combination of duties, however, demanded that she grow. "The work here," Mrs. Knott wrote, "was new to me as an associate editor, which required that I read articles, copy, and proofs all day long, yet as I look back upon it all I would not have missed the experience for anything in the world."[89]

An examination of Mrs. Knott's editorials reveals a writing voice that is unflinching in its strike at the subtlety of error. With beautifully reasoned logic, she could lay out how the discipline of discipleship frees one from the slavery of sense. A Knott editorial could show how obedience to a spiritual demand was not dry, dusty duty, but a pathway that led one out of some mental prison. In a 1904 *Sentinel* editorial, "Self-Denial," for instance, Mrs. Knott showed why it is in one's best interest to counter mortal thought and its suggested selfish mode, and thus to follow Jesus' command to "deny himself":

> *Many have sought to deny themselves, while believing in the*
> *reality of the things given up. We are nowhere told that Jesus*
> *assumed burdens in order to become more spiritual, we are*

told, however, that he was ever removing burdens from the heavy-laden. He was inspired by a lofty purpose, and he knew that in order to fulfil it he must deny himself daily, and take up his cross....

The belief that we are giving up, or "denying" something real, even though it be done from a sense of duty, must ever have a depressing effect; but when we understand that we are only giving up the false for the true, then the "joys of Spirit" beckon us on and on....

The only experiences of this earthly life worth remembering are those in which self has been denied and overcome, for thus alone has true greatness been attained.[90]

Not only did Annie Knott's voice as a writer mature, but she learned that her responsibility as an editor included more than what she had at first assumed. An early rebuke from Mrs. Eddy taught her what it meant to be a sentinel at her post.

On Thursday morning, October 5, 1905, Archibald McLellan, chairman of the Board of Directors and Editor-in-Chief of the periodicals, stood at the door of Mrs. Knott's residence, 106 Gainsborough Street, Boston. He had received a telegram from Mary Baker Eddy that morning, he told Mrs. Knott, instructing the full Board of Directors and the editors of the periodicals to meet Mrs. Eddy at two o'clock that afternoon.

Arriving at Pleasant View seventy miles north of Boston, the Directors and editors were shown upstairs to Mrs. Eddy's office. Chairs were arranged in a semicircle in front of their Leader's desk. Annie Knott was the only woman among the seven visitors.

Mrs. Eddy read aloud the following words from that week's *Christian Science Sentinel:* "a diseased body is not acceptable to God."[91] She addressed each visitor by name and asked each in turn whether the statement was scientific. Mrs. Knott, who was the last to be asked, said that she had stumbled over it twice but had let it stand. Mrs. Eddy then sharply rebuked her, the only one of the three editors who had been taught by Mrs. Eddy. Pointedly reminding Mrs. Knott that she was her student, Mrs. Eddy asked her whether she had taught her "anything like this."[92] Taken aback, Mrs. Knott remained silent, beginning to grasp the gravity of her mistake.

Speaking to the group, Mrs. Eddy asked: "Now, will you any of you tell me whether God has any more use for a well body than for a sick one?"[93] She then candidly told them that "at that very time she was suffering from a belief in illness and that many persons might ask whether God had any use for her when she was manifesting a belief in disease."[94]

While Mrs. Knott bore the brunt of the rebuke, Mrs. Eddy did not spare the others, but told the entire group that she thought they "all ought to have been enough awake to see that it was not a proper statement to send out."[95]

Mrs. Eddy went on to refer to John B. Willis's recent editorial "Watching vs. Watching Out,"[96] explaining to him why it was incorrect but rebuking Annie Knott for allowing the editorial to be published. Until that moment it had not occurred to Mrs. Knott that she was responsible for the correctness of the other editorials, yet she remained silent under the rebuke and offered no defense:

> [*Mrs. Eddy*] *left it very clear that we were each individually responsible for keeping our periodicals distinctly and unmistakably scientific, and that if one made a mistake the others should be sufficiently alert to see that it was corrected.*[97]

The meeting lasted two hours, Mrs. Eddy emphasizing "the great need of keeping the teachings of Christian Science pure, and especially the need of keeping them close to the teachings of Christ Jesus. She said that a false estimate of his mission and his teachings would constitute a serious error; that we must study constantly his teachings and his healing work and endeavor to keep our periodicals up to that high standard."[98]

The following day, when the two associate editors were back in their Boston offices, Mr. Willis came to see Mrs. Knott and apologized for the rebuke she took from Mrs. Eddy because of his editorial. But she scolded him for his apology: "I quickly told him that no one could come between me and my Leader and that what she felt divinely led to give me in the way of rebuke, I would always take with the deepest thankfulness, and I wanted no one's comment upon it."[99]

One wishing to explore the nature of Annie Knott's character and authority as a Christian Scientist need only examine this incident to see the spiritual adroitness and impact of her willingness to accept correction and her refusal to let self-justification shut the door on progress.

The next day Mrs. Knott received a letter from Mrs. Eddy that was dated the same day as their meeting at Pleasant View. Mrs. Eddy must have penned this note soon after the meeting broke up.

"It gives me a hope that the spell is broken and you are awake once more to see your duty and to do it," Mrs. Eddy wrote. "May God bless you abundantly in watching and praying that your temple, 'house', personality, be not broken open."[100]

"It seemed that obedience was the need of the hour"

IN MARCH 1919 MRS. KNOTT ACCEPTED AN APPOINTMENT TO THE CHRISTIAN Science Board of Directors. She was the first woman to hold this position — a remarkable move, since women could not vote in national elections in the United States until the ratification of the Nineteenth Amendment the following year.[101]

In an editorial a decade earlier, "'An Help Meet' for Man," Mrs. Knott wrote that a woman's place in society would progress as the result of the spiritualization of the thought of the people:

Throughout the entire history of the human race we find that woman has been made to hold a subordinate position, whenever and wherever materiality dominated the beliefs of any people. On the other hand, we see that when spirituality has prevailed woman has been accorded her rightful place, at least to the extent of having an opportunity to prove her fitness for sharing in the heroic task of elevating and purifying the race, and thus establishing universal righteousness, with its inevitable harmony and peace.[102]

It was obedience, Mrs. Knott observed, that led her to accept this "opportunity to prove her fitness" for the daunting post of director. "While I shrank from the responsibilities involved in this forward step," she wrote, "it seemed that obedience was the need of the hour, and I at once responded."[103] In a letter to her student and secretary, Helen France, she stated more candidly that she shrank from accepting the assignment "more than from anything I had ever been asked to do, but again I see that the experience has meant more to me than anything else since my childhood up."[104]

We get a glimpse of Mrs. Knott at this point in her life from a note made by a friend after they had spent an evening together, some five months before she joined the Board of Directors. Mary Beecher Longyear described her dinner guest, then in her sixty-ninth year, as "fresh and bright looking and brisk, rather prides herself on her Scottish tendencies . . ." and added, "She works at her desk in the publishing house all day long, looks after her own family — a daughter, married son & wife, and grandson — and teaches a large class of students many from Canada yearly."[105] From this description, to be with Mrs. Knott was to be in the presence of a vigorous and dynamic woman (the photograph of Annie Knott on page 126 was taken at the Longyear home and shows Mrs. Knott with one of Mrs. Longyear's scrapbooks).

On an evening just after she had joined the Board of Directors, Mrs. Knott would find herself drawn into the most severe crisis the church had faced since Mrs. Eddy's passing. A sheriff came to Mrs. Knott's home with a summons ordering her appearance in court to testify, among an array of other witnesses, in the litigation brought in March 1919 by the Trustees of The Christian Science Publishing Society against the Board of Directors. The effect of the suit was to challenge the authority of the *Church Manual.*

But a meeting some twenty-seven years earlier with Mrs. Eddy had, without Mrs. Knott's discerning it at the time, helped to prepare her for this challenge.[106] Mrs. Knott had been in Boston on October 5, 1892, and had joined the newly formed Mother Church on that day. She and her sister Mrs. Stewart were invited to visit Mrs. Eddy, and arriving the following day at Mrs. Eddy's new home, Pleasant View, they met six other Normal students. For two hours Mrs. Eddy unfolded to these students something of the challenges, including legal obstacles, she had faced a few weeks earlier in establishing The Mother Church.

Significantly, one of the eight women Mrs. Eddy was addressing would, nearly three decades later, become a member of the Christian Science Board of Directors and would be able to testify with authority regarding Mrs. Eddy's intent for her church government. Mrs. Knott stated in court that at the October 1892 meeting:

> *Mrs. Eddy said she wanted to have The Mother Church modeled as closely as possible after the early Christian church and after Jesus' teachings, and the Church to be as free as possible from the trammels of material organization. That is the most important thing that I can remember.*[107]

Mrs. Eddy called their attention to the following statement from *Science and Health:*

> *When we realize that there is but one Mind, the divine law of loving our neighbors as ourselves is unfolded to us; whereas a belief in many ruling minds hinders man's normal drift towards the one Mind, one God, and leads human thought into opposite channels, where selfishness reigns.*[108]

Annie M. Knott. Photograph, Charlotte Fairchild, taken at the home of Mary Beecher Longyear in Brookline, Massachusetts, 1918, Longyear Museum Collection.

The decision on the case came the day before Thanksgiving 1921, when the Massachusetts Supreme Judicial Court upheld the authority of the *Church Manual*. Mrs. Knott wrote that the litigation had been "a trying experience, not so much on personal grounds but because of the anxiety lest the Trustees should win the suit which would have been disastrous to our Cause. Happily," she continued, "the point that stands out in memory is that Thanksgiving Day, in 1921, when The Mother Church stood for what it is before the whole world, and was so recognized by the Supreme Court of the Commonwealth of Massachusetts."[109]

Typical of Mrs. Knott's work ethic was the way she took on the demanding job of serving on the Board of Directors. She found within this new task the transformative power of work that takes one beyond what one thinks he or she is capable of. In the process, she discovered fresh perspectives on the Church she so loved:

In my long years of experience I have found that work which at first seems difficult and strenuous becomes altogether joyous and quite easy when we are willing to make the needed effort.... While the work on the Board of Directors is, humanly speaking, the most difficult I have ever undertaken, ... it has given me a broader and deeper sense of the vastness of this movement, and of what has already been accomplished since our Leader stood before the world as the only Christian Scientist.[110]

Despite her strenuous schedule and workload, she still found time to help and heal others. One day, when Mrs. Knott was up against a ticking clock's tight deadline, an eleven-year-old girl who had suffered from epilepsy since childhood was brought down from Maine in the hope of seeing Mrs. Knott. Mrs. Knott was not to be disturbed — but relented once she was told of the case. She lovingly told her visitors that she was unable to take the case, but that she would give them what she could — a treatment of about fifteen minutes.

Mrs. Knott heard nothing more about the case for a year, and then a practitioner stopped by her office and asked for an appointment. Mrs. Knott had asked her secretary, Helen France, to cancel all appointments owing to urgent Board work, but when the visitor mentioned she only had a few minutes, Mrs. Knott agreed to see her. The practitioner sat down and reminded Mrs. Knott of the little Maine girl. She then told her that this girl had been completely healed of epilepsy through Mrs. Knott's single, brief treatment and had been in "perfect health ever since that day."

Their interview expanded from an allotted ten minutes to a full hour, and when it was over, Mrs. France observed that Mrs. Knott's face was "radiant" and there were tears in her eyes. "She said she would not have missed the joy it had brought her for a thousand dollars."[111]

"We always ought to know that Truth is ever at hand," Mrs. Knott said of this event, "and yet we must make the demonstration."[112]

"I have fought a good fight"

AFTER SERVING OVER FOURTEEN YEARS AS A MEMBER OF THE CHRISTIAN
Science Board of Directors, Mrs. Knott resigned early in 1934. Her letter of
resignation read in part:

> This will not come to you as a surprise, since I have made
> known to you for some time my desire for leisure in which to
> gain more of the spirit of Christian Science, and to aid
> others to do the same in larger measure.[113]

Her resignation brought many letters filled with gratitude for Annie M.
Knott's immense contribution. "The only word I can find in the Bible that
seems entirely applicable to your case, though in your humility you would
perhaps be the last to use, is St. Paul's words 'I have fought the good fight,'"
wrote Lyman P. Powell, Episcopalian author of *Mary Baker Eddy: A Life
Size Portrait.*[114]

George Channing, Committee on Publication for Northern California and
later First Reader of The Mother Church, wrote her:

> I am sure that many of the bricks in the structure of the
> Christian Science organization as we know it today have
> been laid by your hands and for this all Christian Scientists
> are grateful.[115]

Francis Lyster Jandron, a Christian Science practitioner and teacher in
Detroit and later a member of the Christian Science Board of Directors,
observed:

> It seems to me that the history of our movement has no
> counterpart for your half-century of distinguished service to
> our Leader in her church. Almost every day someone tells me
> that they learnt the meaning of loyalty from your teaching,
> or your writings, or your work in Michigan.[116]

Annie M. Knott, *far left,* with her family, circa 1893.
Photograph, private collection.

Helen Chaffee Howard (later Elwell) wrote:

How frequently I recall what you said in your Association several years ago: "Enough spiritual joy will solve every problem." ...

Sometime dear Mrs. Knott, I would so appreciate a visit. There are subjects I should love to know more of, the Lesson Sermons for instance, and the Sunday School. Your experience and nearness to our Leader not only render the knowledge invaluable, but indispensable in carrying on the work as our Leader desired.[117]

For seven years after retiring from the Board of Directors, Mrs. Knott was active in her healing practice and in teaching Christian Science.

On Saturday morning, December 20, 1941, Annie Macmillan Knott passed on at her home in Brookline, Massachusetts. Two memorial services were held — one in Boston conducted by George Channing, First Reader of The Mother Church, and the other in Detroit, conducted by the vice president of the association of Mrs. Knott's pupils, George Porter MacMahon.

An article that appeared in *The Boston Herald* the day after her passing observed that Mrs. Knott broke a gender barrier when she became the first woman member of the Christian Science Board of Directors.[118]

But the people whose lives she touched through healing, teaching, and writing may say that the real measure of Mrs. Knott's life was in furthering the coming of the Kingdom of Heaven.

Mrs. Knott's unselfish devotion, strong discipline, and refusal to compromise with error would help set an early standard for spiritual accomplishment and achievement in Christian Science. While Christian Scientists have one Ensample — Christ Jesus[119] — there is much they can learn from examining the lives of devoted and focused students of the Science of Christ like Annie M. Knott, who lived their lives under the New Testament discipline of "not unto themselves."[120]

"The 'life-work' of Annie M. Knott, C.S.D., has been well done," announced Mrs. Knott's Christian Science students' association at the time of her passing, "and she is continuing this work with added joy and freedom because of her faithfulness and obedience."[121]

NOTES

Abbreviations

ET: Emma A. Thompson

ADT: Abigail Dyer Thompson

JW: Janette E. Weller

AMK: Annie Macmillan Knott

LMC: Longyear Museum Collection, Chestnut Hill, Massachusetts

MBEC: The Mary Baker Eddy Collection, The Mary Baker Eddy Library, Boston, Massachusetts

CSJ: The Christian Science Journal

CSS: Christian Science Sentinel

Mary Baker Eddy's published writings: short titles and abbreviations (references are to final editions unless otherwise stated)

Manual: Church Manual of The First Church of Christ, Scientist, in Boston, Mass.

Mis.: Miscellaneous Writings 1883–1896

Miscellany: The First Church of Christ, Scientist, and Miscellany

Pul.: Pulpit and Press

Ret.: Retrospection and Introspection

Science and Health: Science and Health with Key to the Scriptures

Notes to Emma A. Thompson

1. Greer represented Lake City from 1891 to 1895. He also served in the Minnesota State Senate from 1895 to 1903.

2. ADT papers, no date, LMC. The incident took place on a Friday evening in the winter of 1898–99 (ADT to Mary Baker Eddy, May 16, 1899, MBEC). By the 1880s and 1890s, medical communities in many states worked through their legislatures to codify the practice of medicine. This resulted in a series of medical practice acts stipulating the qualifications and requirements of physicians. Some of the pioneer Christian Scientists observed that these laws could have the effect of curtailing the practice of Christian Science, and they challenged their passage. Emma Thompson in Minnesota and Annie Knott in Michigan are two examples.

3. The Primary class, which consisted of twelve lessons, began on August 30, 1886.

4. A month after the class, Mrs. Eddy wrote her: "You must not flinch but go on as you are going strong, calm, meek. Don't get dizzy with human homage; if you do it will tip you over. But you are little in danger, you who wanted to go home because you said you could not honor my College. What did I tell you? Now dear I have great hope and faith in what you will do for our Cause." Mary Baker Eddy to ET, October 16, 1886, L05560, MBEC.

5. ET to Mary Baker Eddy, September 9, 1886, MBEC.

6. ADT, "Memories of Mary Baker Eddy," p. 8, LMC.

7. ADT, two-page statement concerning Emma Thompson and Phineas Quimby, October 14, 1928, MBEC.

8. These classes were: Primary class, August–September 1886; Obstetrics, December 1887; and Normal class, November 1898.

9. ET to Calvin A. Frye, —— 30, 1888, MBEC.

10. ADT papers, "Preface," p. 3, LMC.

11. *CSJ*, vol. 4 (Oct 1886).

12. ET to Mary Baker Eddy, October 5, 1886, MBEC.

13. Venna A. Hale to ADT, October 6, 1946, LMC.

14. Ibid.

15. Lena Steuerwald, typed statement signed, March 1, 1932, LMC.

16. Grace De Vaux to Mrs. Loye, no date, envelope postmarked July 31, 1950, LMC.

17. May E. Bullock to E. L. Jones, March 6, 1898, LMC. After this healing May Bullock took up the study of Christian Science and became a practitioner.

18. Loren Chowen, "Granulated Eyelids,"*CSJ*, vol. 6 (Jan 1889), p. 521.

19. Addie Keith Merrill, typed statement signed, March 1932, p. 1, LMC.

20. Ibid., pp. 2–3.

21. Ibid., pp. 3–4.

22. *Lissette* is the spelling in Lissette Getz's own signature, but elsewhere variations occur, as in this *Journal* entry, where her name is spelled *Lissetta.*

23. L. Getz, "Crutches Discarded,"*CSJ*, vol. 5 (Mar 1888), p. 627.

24. Mary Baker Eddy to ET, March 16, 1887, L05563, MBEC.

25. Mary Baker Eddy notation on envelope containing letter from ET, October 25, 1891, MBEC.

26. Adelaide M. Kinnear, "A Joyous Tribute," *CSJ*, vol. 16 (Apr 1898), pp. 12–13.

27. Ibid.

28. ET to Mary Baker Eddy, July 25, 1888, MBEC.

29. Laura Fox to Longyear Historical Society, September 7, 1972, LMC.

30. ET to Mary Baker Eddy, October 5, 1886, MBEC.

31. Emma Thompson and her daughter Abigail visited Mrs. Eddy from time to time, where they benefitted from Mrs. Eddy's personal instruction.

32. ET to Lissette Getz, August 15, 1890, LMC.

33. Ibid.

34. Mary Baker Eddy to Mary Eaton, October 26, 1900, L04317, MBEC.

35. ADT, "Memories of Mary Baker Eddy," p. 20, LMC.

36. Ibid., p. 28.

37. ET to Mary Baker Eddy, October 5, 1886, MBEC.

38. Mrs. A. Stewart and Nancy Hudec, "The Dumb Speak,"*CSJ*, vol. 6 (Aug 1888), p. 256.

39. *We Knew Mary Baker Eddy* (Boston: The Christian Science Publishing Society, 1979), p. 67.

40. Ibid., pp. 67–68.

41. ADT, "Memories of Mary Baker Eddy," p. 20, LMC.

42. Romans 1:1.

43. Joshua Bailey, notes of Mary Baker Eddy Normal class, May 21, 1889, A10273, MBEC.

44. ET to Mary Baker Eddy, December 5, 1886, MBEC.

45. ET to Mary Baker Eddy, December 12, 1886, MBEC.

46. ET to Mary Baker Eddy, January 13, 1889, MBEC.

47. ADT, one-page typed recollection, unsigned, undated, LMC.

48. ADT, "Sign blown down," p. 2, LMC.

49. See *Science and Health*, p. 583:12–19.

50. ADT, "Memories of Mary Baker Eddy," p. 21, LMC.

51. Adelaide M. Kinnear, "A Joyous Tribute," *CSJ*, vol. 16 (Apr 1898), p. 15.

52. ET to Mary Baker Eddy, October 9, 1898, MBEC.

53. See "Church Dedication in Minneapolis," *CSJ*, vol. 21 (Nov 1903), p. 484.

54. When Fifth and Sixth Churches were formed in 1908, there was a Fourth Church, which apparently disbanded about 1912. Thus, when steps were taken to form another branch in 1915, it became a new Fourth Church.

55. ADT papers, Abbie Y. Stein, "An Excerpt from Clerk's Report, Second Church of Christ, Scientist, Minneapolis, Annual Meeting, February 7, 1935," p. 1, LMC.

56. *Miscellany*, p. 193.

57. Matthew 13:26.

58. ET to Mary Baker Eddy, August 28, 1887, MBEC.

59. ET to Mary Baker Eddy, July 25, 1888, MBEC.

60. ET to Mary Baker Eddy, October 22, 1891, MBEC.

61. ET to Mary Baker Eddy, August 7, 1892, MBEC.

62. Edward J. Brown, M.D., "Letter to the Editor," *Minneapolis Tribune*, September 30, 1887, MBEC.

63. ADT, "Sign blown down," p. 1, LMC.

64. ET to Mary Baker Eddy, December 2, 1888, MBEC.

65. ET to Mary Baker Eddy, October 25, 1886, MBEC.

66. Mary Baker Eddy to ET, October 30, 1886, L05562, MBEC.

67. Mary Baker Eddy to ET, March 16, 1887, L05563, MBEC.

68. ET to Calvin A. Frye, —— 30, 1888, MBEC.

69. ET to Mary Baker Eddy, January 13, 1889, MBEC.

70. Mary Baker Eddy to ET, March 16, 1887, L05563, MBEC.

71. Quoted here from *Mis.*, pp. 58–59.

72. ADT, "Memories of Mary Baker Eddy," p. 8, LMC.

73. Emma Thompson affidavit, February 23, 1907, County of Hennepin, Minnesota, MBEC.

74. ADT, "Memories of Mary Baker Eddy," p. 10, LMC.

75. *Miscellany*, p. 307. See also "Mrs. Eddy Shocked," *Pul.*, pp. 74–75; *Miscellany*, p. 302:18–24; *Manual*, p. 42:11–18.

76. *CSJ*, vol. 4 (Nov 1886), p. 184. In this brief statement Mrs. Thompson mistakenly recalled that her meeting with Mrs. Patterson at Quimby's office occurred in the summer of 1862, whereas Mrs. Patterson first met Quimby on October 10.

77. ET to Mary Baker Eddy, October 22, 1891, MBEC.

78. Mary Baker Eddy to ET, December 30, 1892, L05569, MBEC. Accompanying her gift, Mrs. Thompson wrote: "As every crown gained is a cross lost, may the small emblem indeed prove a crown of blessings and love" (ET to Mary Baker Eddy, December 22, 1892, MBEC).

79. The names of Mary Baker Eddy and the contributors were placed in the corner-stone. See *Mis.*, p. 144.

80. Mary Baker Eddy to ET, March 27, 1894, L05570, MBEC.

81. *Mis.*, p. 143; also *CSJ*, vol. 12 (Jun 1894), pp. 90–93.

82. ADT, "Memories of Mary Baker Eddy," p. 18, LMC.

83. Ibid., p. 20.

84. ET to Calvin A. Frye, —— 30, 1888, MBEC.

85. Daisette Stocking McKenzie reminiscence, p. 50, MBEC.

86. ET to Calvin A. Frye, —— 30, 1888, MBEC.

87. Mary Baker Eddy to ET, December 30, 1892, L05569, MBEC.

NOTES TO ABIGAIL DYER THOMPSON

1. ADT, "Memories of Mary Baker Eddy," p. 34, LMC.

2. Ibid.

3. ADT, Chairman's Report to Second Church of Christ, Scientist, Minneapolis, Minnesota, February 2, 1933, LMC.

4. ADT, "Memories of Mary Baker Eddy," p. 5, LMC.

5. See chapter on Emma A. Thompson.

6. ADT, "Memories of Mary Baker Eddy," p. 22, LMC.

7. ADT to Judge Clifford P. Smith, September 21, 1939, LMC.

8. For details, see We Knew Mary Baker Eddy (Boston: The Christian Science Publishing Society, 1979), pp. 66–68. See also CSS, vol. 34 (Oct 3, 1931), p. 94.

9. ADT, "Memories of Mary Baker Eddy," pp. 5–6, LMC. Mrs. Eddy moved into 385 Commonwealth Avenue the day before Christmas, 1887. She continued to hold classes at the Massachusetts Metaphysical College on Columbus Avenue. Emma Thompson was in Boston to attend the Obstetrics class, which convened on December 5.

10. ADT, "Memories of Mary Baker Eddy," p. 6, LMC.

11. Science and Health, pp. 170–171.

12. Mary Baker Eddy to ADT, June 21, 1896, L05577, MBEC; ADT, "Memories of Mary Baker Eddy," p. 3, LMC.

13. ADT, "Memories of Mary Baker Eddy," p. 26, LMC.

14. ET to Mary Baker Eddy, July 2, 1895, MBEC.

15. ADT to Mary Baker Eddy, April 27, 1897, MBEC.

16. ADT and ET to Mary Baker Eddy, February 10, 1902, MBEC.

17. ADT, "Memories of Mary Baker Eddy," p. 27, LMC. See also We Knew Mary Baker Eddy, p. 66.

18. ADT, "Memories of Mary Baker Eddy," p. 30, LMC. Cf. "Consecration to good does not lessen man's dependence on God, but heightens it" (Science and Health, p. 262).

19. ADT, "Memories of Mary Baker Eddy," pp. 31–32, LMC.

20. ADT, "Memories of Mary Baker Eddy," pp. 32–33, LMC. This experience may have occurred as early as the spring or summer of 1866. Mrs. Eddy specifically states that it was not until the "latter part" of that year that she "gained the scientific certainty that all causation was Mind, and every effect a mental phenomenon" (Ret., p. 24). See also Sue Harper Mims's recollection of the same

incident in *We Knew Mary Baker Eddy,* pp. 132–133. While the two accounts differ in detail, they agree on the major points of the need for humility and that God is the only healer. See also Peter's response to the crowd, who were amazed at the healing of the lame man: "And when Peter saw it, he answered unto the people, … why look ye so earnestly on us, as though by our own power or holiness we had made this man to walk?" (Acts 3:12).

21. ADT to the Christian Science Board of Directors, November 8, 1929, LMC.

22. ADT to Mary Baker Eddy, May 16, 1899, MBEC.

23. William P. Finlay to ADT, May 4, 1927, LMC.

24. ADT papers, LMC.

25. Charles Edward Russell to ADT, November 19, 1925, LMC.

26. ADT papers, LMC.

27. Ruth Kottke to ADT, February 17, 1948, LMC.

28. Interview with Olyn Chapin, January 20, 2004, p. 4, Oral History Project, LMC.

29. Ibid., p. 5.

30. ADT, typed account of her work in obstetrics, p. 1, LMC. This class was taught in Concord, N.H., at Mary Baker Eddy's request. The obstetrics course under the Board of Education was offered from 1899 through 1901, when it was discontinued by Mrs. Eddy.

31. The College of Homeopathic Medicine and Surgery was incorporated and opened at the University of Minnesota in 1886.

32. ADT, typed account of her work in obstetrics, p. 1, LMC.

33. ADT papers, typed account unsigned, September 1931, LMC.

34. See also Philippians 2:14 and Jude 1:16.

35. Olyn Chapin, p. 12, LMC.

36. Interview with Dorothy Ann Hodgman, February 8, 2005, p. 14, Oral History Project, LMC.

37. Ibid., p. 3.

38. Ibid., p. 5.

39. ADT papers, statement signed by Agnes C. DeGroodt, March 1931, p. 1, LMC.

40. ADT papers, statement signed by Mabel DeGroodt, March 1931, p. 1, LMC.

41. ADT papers, Margaret Benson, typed statement signed, August 20, 1942, LMC. The healing occurred in the summer of 1939.

42. ADT to Emma Shipman, April 7, 1942, LMC.

43. ADT to Emma Shipman, May 11, 1942, LMC.

44. Emma Shipman to ADT, May 16, 1942, LMC.

45. *CSS*, vol. 44 (Jul 18, 1942), pp. 1275–1279 and 1281–1284, and *We Knew Mary Baker Eddy*, pp. 63–69 and 139–145.

46. The "Next Friends" suit was brought in Mrs. Eddy's name but against her will, with the objective of gaining control of her property by proving her incompetent to make business decisions. The suit collapsed shortly after a court-ordered examination of Mrs. Eddy at her home established her mental acuity beyond doubt. See Robert Peel, *Mary Baker Eddy: The Years of Authority* (New York: Holt, Rinehart and Winston, 1977), chapter 8, "The World at the Front Door," pp. 253–291.

47. ADT, "Memories of Mary Baker Eddy," pp. 28–29, LMC.

48. Ibid., p. 29.

49. ADT, Chairman's Report to Second Church of Christ, Scientist, Minneapolis, Minnesota, February 2, 1933, LMC.

NOTES TO JANETTE E. WELLER

1. At that time, she was Mrs. F. A. Robinson. To avoid confusion, we have generally referred to her by the name by which she was known through most of her working life as a Christian Scientist.

2. JW, "The Human Side of Mrs. Eddy," 1917, pp. 3–4, MBEC.

3. Ibid., p. 44. Shortly after Mrs. Weller began to study Christian Science, Julia Bartlett spent eleven days in Littleton, healing and giving public talks on Christian Science (see Robert Peel, *Mary Baker Eddy: The Years of Trial* [New York: Holt, Rinehart and Winston, 1971], pp. 147–148). While the two almost certainly met at this time, Mrs. Weller's reminiscence is silent about Julia Bartlett's visit, although there are one or two references to a "Miss B" (presumably Miss Bartlett) in her correspondence.

4. Matthew 7:7.

5. See II Corinthians 5:17.

6. Mary Baker Eddy to JW, November 9, 1888, L13433, MBEC.

7. John 4:10.

8. JW, autobiographical sketch, p. 1, MBEC.

9. JW to Mary Baker Eddy, June 4, 1889, MBEC.

10. Copeland Franklin George Weller passed away on December 8, 1877.

11. JW, "The Human Side," p. 27, MBEC.

12. Fontie passed away on March 5, 1892. JW, autobiographical sketch, p. 3, MBEC.

13. Mary Baker Eddy to JW, June 22, 1886, L13427, MBEC.

14. Mary Baker Eddy to JW, August 1, 1895, L13448, MBEC.

15. JW, "The Human Side," p. 6, MBEC.

16. Ibid., pp. 6–7.

17. Ibid., p. 31.

18. Mary Baker Eddy to JW, March 29, 1896, L13453, MBEC.

19. JW, "The Human Side," p. 7, MBEC.

20. Ibid.

21. See Luke 10:17.

22. *No and Yes*, p. 13.

23. Mrs. Baker had served as a Congregationalist missionary among the Choctaw Indians and maintained an enduring love for her sister-in-law. Mrs. Eddy turned to Mrs. Weller when Mrs. Baker needed practical care during her last years.

24. The class commenced on March 29, 1886.

25. JW, "The Human Side," p. 19, MBEC.

26. Ibid., p. 19.

27. JW to Calvin A. Frye, July 19, 1888, MBEC.

28. See Matthew 7:14.

29. JW, "The Human Side," p. 6, MBEC.

30. Mary Baker Eddy to JW, January 26, 1885, L13426, MBEC.

31. Mary Baker Eddy to JW, March 23, 1887, L13428, MBEC.

32. Mary Baker Eddy to JW, September 24, 1895, L13451, MBEC. See also *Mis.*, pp. 54:25–55:15.

33. Janette Weller dictated her reminiscence, "The Human Side of Mrs. Eddy," during the summer of 1917. This narrative, written in her mid-seventies, recounts many of her experiences working for and visiting with Mrs. Eddy. Mary Beecher Longyear met Mrs. Weller in 1918 and noted that she "had a beautiful face but there was fire in her eyes" (Mary Beecher Longyear diary, March 6, 1918, LMC).

34. Mrs. S. E. Barnum, "Rheumatism in a Girl," *CSJ*, vol. 6 (May 1888), p. 92.

35. JW, "The Human Side," pp. 24–25, MBEC.

36. Ibid., p. 25.

37. Mary Baker Eddy to JW, December 23, 1893, L13434, MBEC.

38. JW to Calvin A. Frye, June 9, 1896, MBEC.

39. JW to Mary Baker Eddy, May 3, 1895, MBEC.

40. *Science and Health*, p. 66.

41. JW, "The Human Side," p. 30, MBEC.

42. JW, "The Human Side," p. 32, MBEC.

43. Ibid., p. 8.

44. Ibid., p. 11. See also *Miscellany*, pp. 314–315, for statement concerning Daniel Patterson made by R. D. Rounsevel, Mrs. Weller's brother-in-law.

45. JW, seven-page untitled reminiscence, p. 4, MBEC.

46. Ibid., p. 5.

47. *Miscellany*, p. 185.

48. Mary Baker Eddy to JW, September 24, 1895, L13451, MBEC.

49. JW, "The Human Side," p. 35, MBEC.

50. Mary Baker Eddy to JW, August 28, 1894, L13439, MBEC.

51. JW to Mary Baker Eddy, August 15, 1901, MBEC.

52. JW, "The Human Side," p. 39, MBEC.

53. *Miscellany*, p. 197. Other examples could be given, such as: "Let there be milk for babes, but let not the milk be adulterated. Unless this method be pursued, the Science of Christian healing will again be lost, and human suffering will increase" (*Ret.*, pp. 61–62).

54. JW to Mary Baker Eddy, March 22, 1907, MBEC.

NOTES TO ANNIE M. KNOTT

1. The doctor consulted another physician, who concurred with the prognosis.

2. Two years earlier Annie M. Knott had written to Mrs. Eddy on May 27, 1885, that newspapers were publishing attacks on Christian Science.

3. *We Knew Mary Baker Eddy* (Boston: The Christian Science Publishing Society, 1979), p. 74. Mrs. Knott made this statement regarding another healing that occurred at about the same time, that of a violently insane man (see pp. 100–101).

4. AMK, "Reminiscences" (article), *CSJ*, vol. 18 (Feb 1901), p. 683.

5. AMK reminiscences, sec. 1, p. 10, MBEC.

6. Matthew 7:7.

7. AMK, "Reminiscences" (article), *CSJ*, vol. 18, p. 680; AMK reminiscences, sec. 1, p. 3, MBEC.

8. AMK to Mary Baker Eddy, May 27, 1885, MBEC.

9. AMK reminiscences, sec. 1, p. 1, MBEC.

10. AMK to Mary Baker Eddy, May 27, 1885, MBEC. Mrs. Knott described the insensitive conduct of two medical practitioners to whom she had turned when her infant son was ill and passed on in England: "During the illness of my child Dr. Hahnemann, the grandson of the founder of the homeopathic system and himself an eminent physician, was employed. As Dr. Hahnemann was suddenly called away an allopathic doctor was summoned, who began to congratulate the agonized mother upon her change of schools, saying that no homeopathic doctor could sign a death certificate in England at that time (1881). When Dr. Hahnemann returned in a day or two he called and said that it would be useless for him to resume the treatment, as the remedies employed by the allopathic physician were sufficient to kill a young child, and that the case was hopeless now. He admitted also that, although he was a graduate of several colleges, he could not sign a death certificate. The child died, but the whole sad experience prepared the way for the acceptance of Christian Science, which came at a time of great need, and soon after the return to this country [the United States]. It is indeed strange, in view of the wide extent of human misery, the almost universal want and woe, that all the world does not help to remove every barrier which stands in the way of the alleviation of its ceaseless suffering" (AMK lecture on April 12, 1899, in *CSJ*, vol. 17 [Jun 1899], p. 163).

11. Christian Friedrich Samuel Hahnemann (1755–1843).

12. Charles Haddon Spurgeon (1834–1892). Spurgeon's sermons are still popular today.

13. AMK reminiscences, sec. 1, p. 2, MBEC. Mrs. Knott did not specify whether this "glimpse" was an intuitive sense of the truth which she later found in Christian Science or whether it was direct contact with Christian Science.

14. AMK, "Reminiscences" (article), *CSJ*, vol. 18, p. 681.

15. AMK reminiscences, sec. 1, pp. 3–4, MBEC. Soon after this healing, Mrs. Knott herself began to receive calls for healing.

16. AMK, "Reminiscences" (article), *CSJ*, vol. 18, p. 681.

17. AMK reminiscences, sec. 1, p. 4, MBEC.

18. AMK, "Reminiscences" (article), *CSJ*, vol. 18, pp. 681–682.

19. AMK reminiscences, sec. 1, p. 4, MBEC.

20. AMK, "Reminiscences" (article), *CSJ,* vol. 41 (Mar 1924), p. 595.

21. AMK to Mary Baker Eddy, May 27, 1885, MBEC.

22. AMK to Mary Baker Eddy, September 10, 1888, MBEC.

23. AMK reminiscences, sec. 1, pp. 5–6, MBEC.

24. After a San Francisco Christian Scientist, Arthur Fosbery, compiled a list of healings supposedly accomplished by Mrs. Eddy and gave Mrs. Knott a copy, she wrote him that she was "not very sympathetic" with his efforts, as she herself knew firsthand that some of the healings on his list were not correct. AMK to Arthur F. Fosbery, January 24, 1931, MBEC.

25. AMK remarks to Board of Lectureship and the Christian Science Board of Directors, June 7, 1928, LMC.

26. AMK reminiscences, sec. 1, p. 8, MBEC.

27. Ibid.

28. Ibid., sec. 2, p. 1.

29. Ibid.

30. On the letterhead Mary's surname was printed as "McMillan," but this was corrected in the *Journal* listing to read "Macmillan."

31. AMK reminiscences, sec. 1, p. 9, MBEC. In her early practice, Mrs. Eddy herself also felt awe before divine Mind's omnipotence, writing in the first edition of *Science and Health* (1875): "We have actually stood in awe at the absolute might of Truth, when witnessing the effect a little has on the sick, and sadly remembered how much could be done by the truly wise, 'who put oil in their lamps' and have not the power to abuse the science of being" (p. 373).

32. Mary Baker Eddy to AMK, March 19, 1887, L04736, MBEC.

33. Mary Baker Eddy to AMK, August 29, 1888, L04739, MBEC.

34. Memo by Lucia Warren, August 21, 1930, signed by AMK on November 4, 1937, MBEC. Mrs. Webster had known Mrs. Eddy's sister Abigail Tilton, from whom she had acquired a prejudice against Mrs. Eddy and Christian Science.

35. Regarding healing when the patient has no faith in Christian Science, see *Science and Health*, p. 358:24–10, and *Mis.*, p. 33:12–20.

36. AMK to Mary Baker Eddy, December 28, 1888, MBEC. See also "News from

Abroad," *CSJ*, vol. 6 (Feb 1889), pp. 588–589, and "News from Abroad,"
CSJ, vol. 7 (May 1889), pp. 103–104. Interestingly, when Annie Knott's letter to
"a friend in Boston" (Mrs. Eddy) was published in the February 1889 *Journal*,
she was so little known among Christian Scientists that the editor assumed that
"A. M. Knott" was a man and referred to her as "Bro. Knott."

37. *Science and Health*, p. 456.

38. AMK reminiscences, sec. 5, p. 5, MBEC. About a year later, Mrs. Knott received a
similar call from another young woman. She sensed the nature of the underlying
error and told the patient so. "The patient admitted it," Mrs. Knott wrote, "and to
human sense there was little or no hope of her recovery, but I did not leave the
house that night until the error was overcome" (AMK reminiscences, sec. 5, p. 6,
MBEC). This young woman also was completely healed.

39. AMK to Mary Baker Eddy, August 28, 1895, MBEC. See also *Science and Health*,
pp. 84–85; p. 94:24–18. Mrs. Knott relates the incident regarding the child who
had swallowed the penny in her reminiscences, sec. 5, pp. 4–5, MBEC.

40. AMK reminiscences, sec. 5, p. 5, MBEC.

41. AMK, "To the Mayor and Citizens of Detroit, in the Year 2001, Greeting,"
December 31, 1900. See also *CSS*, vol. 103, no. 12 (Mar 19, 2001), pp. 18–19.
When the city of Detroit sealed their "Century Box" in 1900, Annie M. Knott was
among the just-over fifty Detroit citizens invited to include an open letter to be
read a century later.

42. AMK reminiscences, sec. 2, pp. 5–6, MBEC. Mrs. Eddy recognized that healing
does not necessarily result in a patient's becoming a student of Christian Science
(see *No and Yes*, p. 40:23–27). In October 1888, when Mrs. Knott was in Mrs.
Eddy's class in obstetrics, Mrs. Eddy asked Mrs. Knott outside of the classroom one
day about her work in these kinds of cases. When Mrs. Knott told her teacher of
this unusual case and the resulting healing, Mrs. Eddy repeated it in class and
mentioned Mrs. Knott's name, to her surprise.

43. *Science and Health*, p. 97.

44. AMK report to the Christian Science Board of Directors, Trustees of The Christian
Science Publishing Society, Editors, et al., September 5, 1928, MBEC.

45. AMK to Mary Baker Eddy, May 7, 1897, MBEC.

46. Ibid.

47. Mary Baker Eddy to AMK, May 10, 1897, L04745, MBEC.

48. In a sermon, Mrs. Eddy observed that her "Early training, through the misinterpre-
tation of the Word, had been the underlying cause of the long years of invalidism
she endured before Truth dawned upon her understanding, through right interpretation. With the understanding of Scripture-meanings, had come physical rejuve-
nation. The uplifting of spirit was the upbuilding of the body" (*Mis.*, p. 169).

49. AMK reminiscences, sec. 1, p. 17, MBEC.

50. AMK reminiscences, sec. 2, p. 7, MBEC. While biblical scholarship has progressed beyond these titles and many of their assumptions and conclusions have been superseded, these volumes influenced the biblical education of several generations. Interestingly, Abbott's grandson, Willis Abbot, was a member of The Mother Church and became editor of *The Christian Science Monitor* in 1922. R. Chenevix Trench is the author of the text of hymn 182 in the *Christian Science Hymnal.*

51. *We Knew Mary Baker Eddy,* p. 79.

52. AMK to Helen Erskine (later France), January 16, 1925, MBEC.

53. AMK to Mary Baker Eddy, December 7, 1888, MBEC.

54. AMK to Mary Baker Eddy, May 21, 1896, MBEC.

55. *CSS,* vol. 103, no. 12 (Mar 19, 2001), p. 19.

56. AMK to Mary Baker Eddy, December 9, 1897, MBEC.

57. "Dedication of Church at Detroit," *CSJ,* vol. 16 (Apr 1898), p. 16.

58. AMK to the Mayor and Citizens of Detroit, December 31, 1900, Detroit Historical Society.

59. *CSJ,* vol. 16 (Apr 1898), p. 17.

60. Ibid., p. 20. See also *Miscellany,* p. 183.

61. AMK to Mary Baker Eddy, September 10, 1888, MBEC.

62. AMK reminiscences, sec. 2, p. 3, MBEC.

63. AMK address to Committees on Publication, October 7, 1921, LMC.

64. AMK, "The Study of the Manual," *CSS,* vol. 7 (Dec 17, 1904), p. 248.

65. Mary Baker Eddy to AMK, November 15, 1906, L04757, MBEC.

66. "Remarks by Mrs. Annie M. Knott at Conference of the Board of Lectureship with The Christian Science Board of Directors," June 7, 1928, LMC.

67. AMK to Mary Baker Eddy, August 28, 1895, MBEC. The students who were causing Mrs. Knott such trouble were the exception, as elsewhere she commented on how wrenching it was for her to leave the large number of her loving students in Detroit when she was called to Boston in 1903 to become Associate Editor (AMK to Helen France, December 19, 1924, quoted by Helen France in an unpublished address, private collection).

68. AMK to Mary Baker Eddy, May 21, 1896, MBEC.

69. AMK to Mary Baker Eddy, June 4, 1896, MBEC.

70. Mary Baker Eddy to AMK, June 16, 1896, L04744, MBEC.

71. *Science and Health,* p. 66.

72. When Mary Beecher Longyear's daughter Judith passed on in 1924, Mrs. Knott sent a letter of comfort: "Last evening I had a call from Mrs. [Frances Thurber] Seal of New York, who informed me of the passing on of your dear daughter, Judith. I can assure you that my thought went to you with a deep sense of love and sympathy in this experience, for I know so well what it must mean to you, even with our unfolding sense of man's immortality as a child of God. The word also recalled my own experience of a good many years ago, when my beloved daughter passed on. Although she was perhaps dearer to me than anyone on this plane, I had such a marvelous sense of the deathless life come to me at that hour that I could see that she had stepped forward into clearer light than we had realized here, and so I was able to comfort others...."

"In spite of the world's very disturbing condition at this time, I feel that the kingdom of God, with all its blessings, is nearer humanity than ever before, and that the hard lessons of human experience, especially those which come through our human affections, will prepare us to appreciate more fully the blessings which come with a closer realization of man's immortality."

Mrs. Knott closed her letter to Mrs. Longyear: "We need have no regrets for the dear ones who pass on, and as we grow wiser we shall not hold any regrets for ourselves but learn the lessons of Love" (AMK to Mary Beecher Longyear, October 10, 1924, LMC).

73. *CSJ*, vol. 23 (Sep 1905), p. 395. Many of Mrs. Knott's articles contain passages that, in the light of her life history, suggest that she is writing from experience. For example, the following excerpt from a 1903 article, "Lessons from the Past and Present," reads: "It is well for us to remember, if we are ever tempted to think that our burdens are heavy, that others have been tried even more than we, and let us honestly put into the scales of experience our countless blessings, and see if we have not what Paul called, 'a far more exceeding and eternal weight of glory.' If we are to be tried in the furnace, let us go without fear into the purifying flames, and remember the three Hebrews who were untouched by the fire, save that the fetters which bound them were consumed. There is no victory so great as this, — to pass through every seeming danger unharmed, and thus to know at length what Science teaches, the utter powerlessness of evil" (*CSJ*, vol. 21 [Jun 1903], p. 162).

74. *Science and Health*, p. 265.

75. AMK single-paragraph account dated June 7, 1923, MBEC. See also AMK reminiscences, sec. 5, p. 2, MBEC.

76. AMK reminiscences, sec. 5, p. 2, MBEC.

77. Ibid.

78. Ibid., p. 3.

79. *We Knew Mary Baker Eddy*, p. 82.

80. *Sheboygan Daily Journal.* Reprinted in *CSS*, vol. 1, no. 26 (Feb 23, 1899), p. 9.

81. Abridged from a fragment of a notebook in which Mrs. Knott kept a record of expenses and receipts, LMC. Mrs. Knott's handwritten notes record, for example, that the train fare from Detroit to Kansas City was $19.00, sleeper accommodation $3.75, and meals $1.50.

82. Thomas Hatten to Mary Baker Eddy, July 6, 1903, with her written notation, L17055, MBEC.

83. Some years later Mrs. Knott was able to resume teaching. Regarding income from her lecturing, in 1899 churches generally paid her $50 per lecture, as recorded in the fragment of the notebook cited in note 81.

84. Mary Baker Eddy to Thomas Hatten, July 9, 1903, L07240, MBEC.

85. AMK to the Christian Science Board of Directors, January 31, 1934, MBEC.

86. Mary Baker Eddy to AMK, August 31, 1903, L04749, MBEC.

87. Mary Baker Eddy to AMK, October 27, 1903, L04750, MBEC.

88. AMK reminiscences, sec. 5, p. 3, MBEC.

89. AMK to Helen France, December 19, 1924, quoted in an unpublished address by Helen France, p. 9, private collection.

90. AMK, "Self-Denial," *CSS*, vol. 6 (Jan 30, 1904), p. 344.

91. Clarence Chadwick, "'The redemption of our body,'" *CSS*, vol. 8 (Sep 30, 1905), p. 67.

92. *We Knew Mary Baker Eddy*, p. 84.

93. Ibid., pp. 84–85. At this meeting Mrs. Eddy "insisted that man's likeness to God is never a physical likeness" and referred her visitors to *Science and Health*, p. 313:12–19.

94. AMK reminiscences, sec. 5, p. 9, MBEC. It is understandable how the negative impact of such thoughts could add to what Mrs. Eddy was dealing with.

95. *Proceedings in Equity 1919–1921 Concerning Deed of Trust of January 25, 1898, Constituting The Christian Science Publishing Society* (Boston: The Christian Science Publishing Society, 1921), p. 646.

96. *CSS*, vol. 8 (Sep 16, 1905), pp. 40–41. Mrs. Eddy's correction of this editorial may be found in *Miscellany*, pp. 232–233.

97. AMK reminiscences, sec. 5, p. 10, MBEC.

98. *Proceedings in Equity*, p. 646. The court report styled the pronouns referring to Christ Jesus as uppercase; they have been styled lowercase here to conform to Mrs. Eddy's usage.

99. AMK reminiscences, sec. 5, p. 10, MBEC.

100. Mary Baker Eddy to AMK, October 5, 1905, L04755, MBEC.

101. In a 1914 editorial, "Greetings," Annie Knott wrote: "In the sixteenth chapter of Paul's epistle to the Romans we find a deeply interesting review of the spiritual history of that time. We discover in this chapter no trace of prejudice against the

ministry of women; on the contrary, there are numerous references to them as fellow workers with the apostles, Phebe receiving this high commendation, 'She hath been a succorer of many.' The names of both men and women, as found in this chapter, would indicate that they were of different nationalities, but the one thing which bound them to Paul and to one another was the fact that they were 'in Christ,' and with touching humility Paul says that some of them were in Christ before he was" (CSS, vol. 17 [Nov 28, 1914], pp. 250–251).

102. CSS, vol. 11 (May 1, 1909), p. 691.

103. We Knew Mary Baker Eddy, p. 86.

104. Quoted in Helen France, address, p. 9, private collection.

105. Mary Beecher Longyear diary, October 10, 1918, LMC.

106. Three weeks before she testified in court, Mrs. Knott wrote Mrs. Longyear: "I hope to give testimony which will be an important link in the history of our movement, because it will hold to the direct line of evidence as to what our Leader said to me in the presence of seven women students on one occasion [October 6, 1892], and the whole Board of Directors and the editors on another occasion [October 5, 1905]." AMK to Mary Beecher Longyear, July 9, 1919, LMC. In her court testimony given July 30, Mrs. Knott did provide information about these two meetings with Mrs. Eddy.

107. Proceedings in Equity, p. 644. Two years later, Mrs. Knott provided additional information about the October 1892 meeting at a conference of Committees on Publication:

"I wish you all could have heard what she [Mrs. Eddy] had to say to us about the working out of this great church. She spoke a good deal about the difficulties which she had had to encounter from the opposition of even friendly lawyers, who told her that this form of organization [that is, the one Mrs. Eddy had just established for her church] was quite impossible, contrary to precedent, and unprovided for in human law. But she worked and prayed until at length, as you have all heard many times, a statute was discovered by one of her lawyers which made this form of organization possible [see first numbered paragraph of the Deed of Trust, September 1, 1892, Manual, p. 130]. She was very happy indeed that the work could go on unobstructed from that time. After speaking of this, she spent the rest of the afternoon in telling us of the many attacks which were being made by mortal mind, through its many avenues or channels, for the destruction of this movement. She said some things which were so startling that at the close of her remarks she asked us never to speak of these things to anyone. And so, even at this late date, I will forbear; but I think there is nothing wrong in saying that mortal mind exercises all its ingenuity in attempts made through legal and legislative ways to make Christian Science not only impossible, but its practice punishable, in ways of which I must not now speak. When she had told us all this, warned us in this way, her face brightened up and she said, 'You must never fear evil, no matter what the seeming may be.' ... And then at the close of her remarks, before she said goodbye to us on that occasion, she said words which you have often heard quoted. They were these: 'If you, my dear students, could but see the grandeur of your outlook, the infinitude of your hope, and the infinite capabilities of your being, you would do what? You would let error destroy itself.'" ("Mrs. Knott's Address at the Conference of Committees on Publication, October 7, 1921," LMC.)

108. *Science and Health*, 70th edition, 1892, p. 101 (see p. 205 of final edition). Mrs. Knott observed: "As she read this to us from our inspired textbook, it seemed as if those few lines alone furnished the rule for working out every human problem, no matter how difficult it might seem, and especially the marvelous words, 'man's normal drift towards the one Mind, one God.' Her wonderful understanding rang out in every word as she read this passage. She pointed out to us without hesitation, as Christ Jesus had done in his day, the attacks of error to which her followers would be subjected, but at the same time she reminded us constantly of the utter powerlessness of error to hinder the progress of Christian Science" (*We Knew Mary Baker Eddy*, p. 80).

109. AMK to the Christian Science Board of Directors, January 31, 1934, MBEC.

110. From a letter quoted in "Mrs. Annie M. Knott, C.S.D., A Brief Account of Her Work for the Cause of Christian Science" (no publisher, no date), p. 8.

111. Helen France, address, pp. 20–21, private collection.

112. Ibid., p. 21.

113. AMK to the Christian Science Board of Directors, January 4, 1934, quoted in *CSJ*, vol. 51 (Mar 1934), p. 680.

114. Lyman P. Powell to AMK, January 6, 1934, private collection. Lyman Powell is citing II Timothy 4:7: "I have fought a good fight, I have finished my course, I have kept the faith."

115. George Channing to AMK, January 9, 1934, private collection.

116. Francis L. Jandron to AMK, January 20, 1934, private collection.

117. Helen Chaffee Howard to AMK, January 25, 1934, private collection. Regarding Mrs. Howard's desire to learn more about the Sunday School and Bible Lesson work, it is interesting to note that she would serve five years as Assistant Superintendent of The Mother Church Sunday School, until 1940, when she was appointed to the Bible Lesson Committee. From 1944 to 1947 she was Second Reader of The Mother Church, and served a year's term as President of The Mother Church, 1947–48, after which she was reappointed to the Bible Lesson Committee, serving until 1961.

118. *The Boston Herald*, December 21, 1941.

119. *Manual*, Art. VIII, Sec. 3, p. 41.

120. I Peter 1:12.

121. Letter from "Association of Students in Christian Science, Mrs. Annie M. Knott, C.S.D., Teacher," to members of the Association, December 30, 1941, LMC.